PARDON OF INNOCENCE

A MEMOIR

PARDON OF INNOCENCE

An Inspiring Story of Faith and Freedom

LIEUTENANT GENERAL MICHAEL T. FLYNN
U.S. ARMY (RETIRED)

BOMBARDIER
BOOKS

Published by Bombardier Books
An Imprint of Post Hill Press
ISBN: 979-8-89565-181-0
ISBN (eBook): 979-8-89565-182-7

Pardon of Innocence:
An Inspiring Story of Faith and Freedom
© 2025 by Lieutenant General Michael T. Flynn, U.S. Army (Retired)
All Rights Reserved

Cover Design by Cody Corcoran

Post Hill Press
New York • Nashville
posthillpress.com

Published in the United States of America
1 2 3 4 5 6 7 8 9 10

DISCLAIMER

In the interest of national security, confidentiality, and legal compliance, certain portions of this book contain redacted material. These redactions were made in consultation with relevant authorities to protect classified information, sensitive discussions, and the privacy of individuals.

While every effort has been made to maintain the integrity and accuracy of the narrative, the redacted content may occasionally affect the completeness of specific events or conversations. Nevertheless, the spirit and essence of the story remain true to the author's experiences and the historical context in which they unfolded.

Readers should understand that the redactions do not alter the core message of this memoir but reflect a necessary balance between transparency and responsibility.

TABLE OF CONTENTS

ACKNOWLEDGMENTS

I DEDICATE THIS BOOK TO my wife Lori, who is not only my wife, but my best friend, confidant, and steadfast supporter, and has been all of these throughout our entire life's journey. From our early days as teenagers, to our long and challenging decades of numerous military experiences, we have lived ten lifetimes but still enjoy walking hand in hand along the shores of life. Thank you for your love and strength during these many challenging and difficult years. I always say if you want a lifetime of happiness, you must like the one you love. Our relationship was tested many times, but our faith in God and each other gave us the strength to continue on the path of equal justice for all.

To my two sons Michael and Matthew, who are such an integral part of this story. You both deserve to know and carry on the truth. Your inner strength and faith in God and in each other have brought a strength and courage to our family and those around you that is limitless.

To my grandchildren, you are the reason I do what I do in this life, and the reason why history needed to be recorded and corrected. I love you all.

To my brothers and sisters who have also felt the brunt of my persecution. You have been loyal, protective, and outspoken about the injustices that occurred this past decade. If there was ever a doubt about the fighting Irish, the phrase "Fight Like a Flynn" demonstrates once again how our strong Irish family came together and stood up against the greatest odds and the greatest threats freedom ever faced and hands down defeated it!

To the millions of Americans who stood by my side and my family's side from day *one*, with prayers, words of encouragement, cards, letters, rosary beads, donations to my Legal Defense Fund, texts, social media posts and so many other heartfelt gestures, it meant the world to me and got my family through some tough times.

In the end, faith, family and true friends won the day and we as a family are stronger because of all three.

FOREWORD
By Lee Smith

THE STORY YOU'RE ABOUT TO read is one of the most important in American history. The story of Michael Flynn is about a good man who was punished though he did nothing wrong, a man who served his country in war abroad and was outflanked at home by maniacal, powerful forces. The government he served turned against him while the American people rushed to his side and linked arms with his family to defend him. Flynn's enemies, his hunters, tried to beat him down for good, but he got up every time, gathering strength each time he stood. It's the sort of thing you see in a classic Western movie. It's what Americans are supposed to learn about character, virtue, and courage watching movies or reading books about heroes. And this is a story about an American hero.

It starts like a story you'd hear at a high school reunion. Mike Flynn—terrific athlete, real daredevil, surfer, lifeguard, a little bit of a troublemaker before his girlfriend Lori Andrade straightened him out. She's from a big Portuguese family in Middletown, Rhode Island, like the Flynns, the big Irish family in the small cottage on the beach. Lori and Mike married, and the Army commissioned him as a second lieutenant in 1981. He fought in Grenada, the first major US combat mission after Vietnam, restoring American prestige and showing Moscow that Ronald Reagan was serious about rolling back communism. And Grenada is where Mike Flynn stepped into his fate when he jumped off a cliff and swam out to save two soldiers who were drifting out to sea.

His commanding officers were not happy with his decision to take matters into his own hands. He might have called in a rescue team. But who knows if those soldiers would have survived the delay? It seems that for Flynn there was no other choice, as if his nature had determined his action. If you were watching it in a movie, or reading it in a book, this is when you'd first recognize that this is about something different, something special, a story about doing good no matter what it costs.

In the immediate aftermath of 9/11, Michael Flynn goes to war in Iraq and Afghanistan, where he becomes the top intelligence officer of his generation. It turns out that what he learned on the bad side of town in a small working-class New England city has applications in tough neighborhoods on the other side of the world. His ideas for fixing how the US collects intelligence in theater and gets it to the warfighters in the field changes the course of the Iraq war. Back in Washington, half the intelligence bureaucracy wants to string him up and others want to crown him.

In 2010, Flynn, now a general, is summoned to the American capital and urged to implement his ideas about stealing our enemies' secrets and safeguarding our own. He's eventually named director of the Defense Intelligence Agency, a post in which, once again, his path is determined by choices that are inseparable from his character.

As DIA director, Flynn testifies in front of Congress about the threats facing America. He says that, contrary to the political talking points coming out of the White House, Islamic terrorists are not on the run, they're as dangerous as ever. In Washington, where politics and posturing take precedence over clarity and conscience, telling the truth is not how things are done. Having reached the inner sanctum of American power, almost anyone else would do anything to preserve his privilege and advance his position. In telling the truth, Flynn stays true to himself and is pushed out of his job.

He leaves government and retires from the US Army after thirty-three years in uniform. In the private sector, he's glad to be working with his son Michael and keen to continue alerting Americans to the threats facing our country. He gives public talks, makes media appearances, and advises presidential candidates preparing for the 2016 race. He hits it off with outsider candidate Donald Trump, a billionaire celebrity with no experience in politics but who sees the world, and America, the way Flynn does. The retired three-star general campaigns with Trump to help him contest what seems the nearly inevitable presidency of Hillary Clinton. When Trump defeats the establishment's choice, the Leviathan commits to fighting the new commander-in-chief to the end.

The columns arrayed against the new administration—a consortium including US intelligence services, big tech, and media—are led by Trump's predecessor, Barack Obama, who warns the president-elect not to hire the adviser he's come to trust most, Michael Flynn. In fact, this is not a warning but a vow—to get Trump, Obama means to come after Flynn first. Obama and his vice president, later president, Joe Biden plot against the incoming national security advisor and deploy the FBI, the ruling establishment's praetorian guard, to take him out. Within weeks of Trump's inauguration, his national security advisor, Michael Flynn, is gone from the White House.

None of it makes sense, not even at the time, amid the frenzied media storm driven by corruption and rancor to destabilize the American government. No foreign adversary could have run a more destructive campaign of information warfare targeting our nation. To get Flynn, the ruling class set chaos loose and turned reason on its head. Flynn was under suspicion because he spoke with the Russian ambassador? But the job of the national security advisor is to speak with foreign officials. How is that a problem, except in a city like Washington that's lost its mind? Flynn lied to the FBI? That makes no sense—it's not in his character. Flynn was forced from the DIA because after his superiors edited his testimony and effectively directed him to lie to Congress; he ignored the consequences and told the truth. But now he chooses to lie?

In the following pages, Flynn describes what it was like for him at this time, like the sensation of going under, as if he were beaten by waves, swallowed up by the ocean, and drowning at the bottom. Very few will ever suffer what Michael Flynn endured, and history shows that most who do are broken by the furies unleashed against them.

Those who come out stronger and wiser, sharpened and made finer by ordeal, are rare. The stories told about those who go down and rise more resolute than before are the stories that civilizations tell to instruct their children in character, virtue, and courage. These are the stories that encapsulate a nation's legacy and are passed from generation to generation. And it's worth remarking that in these stories, the heroes all experience that same going under that Flynn describes. It's an essential component of their journey. The ancient Greeks had a word for it, *katabasis*—the descent.

The protagonist of the *Odyssey* is a warrior trying to get home from years of foreign war. The wily Odysseus is credited not only for his fighting skills but also his stratagems. It was he came up with the idea of fooling the Trojans into believing that the Greeks had abandoned the fight and left to their foes a gift in tribute—the Trojan horse. Odysseus, the man of many devices, is essentially an intelligence officer, the greatest of his generation. To make his way home, he goes down to the underworld, where he's again tested before he's granted the guidance he seeks to return to the wife and son and country he hasn't seen in twenty years. In the *Aeneid*, the Roman hero goes down to walk among the shades to speak with his late father about the great nation he is destined to found, Rome. And in the Italians' great story, Dante must go through the inferno, hell, before he can rise to the light, paradise.

Michael Flynn's story of course isn't an epic poem. It's real, and it's the story of a real man made of flesh and blood. And so what he found when he went down wasn't a vision of the underworld but real people, Americans. He relates in this account of his life how Americans went down with him, to take his hand, and help him breathe. Thousands, then tens of thousands, and now hundreds of thousands of his fellow citizens sent him cards and letters to express their gratitude and love—and they asked him for guidance. Flynn writes here that he was surprised at first to find that during the midst of his ordeal they looked to him for inspiration. They helped him get back to the surface, and in his ascent he pulled up with him all those who also sought the light.

This heroic story then is also about the nobility and goodness of Americans who embody the qualities that stories about men of character, virtue, and courage instill in us. Michael Flynn's story is one Americans will pass down through the generations.

CHAPTER 1

RAZOR'S EDGE

THE COUP STARTED IN THE Oval Office. It's easy to remember when it started—exactly four years and a day before Americans gathered in Washington to protest the widespread election fraud that threw the 2020 election to Joe Biden. If you believe the Democrats, their media allies, and their corrupt partners in our national security establishment, January 6, 2021, was a day of infamy. As bad as Pearl Harbor. Biden said it was as bad as the Civil War. But it was just Americans exercising their First Amendment rights and liberties that our founding fathers and generations fought and died for. No, the real insurrection, the war against the Constitution, started on January 5, 2017, in a meeting to discuss how to deal with me.

This is where the story of my life first meets and intersects with one of the darkest chapters in our nation's history. That's the story of how Barack Obama mustered his considerable forces inside and outside the federal government to undermine and delegitimize his successor, Donald Trump. I was the new president's national security advisor (NSA), counseling him on the dangers to America abroad and at home.

We'd spent the better part of the past year traveling together on the campaign trail. We spoke regularly. I spoke frankly about the dangers to our peace and prosperity. Candidate Trump appreciated my insights on foreign adversaries like China, Russia, and Iran as well as terrorists that targeted the American homeland. I respected his deep love for America and his strong desire to get it right. He knew we'd been on the wrong track for years and wanted to make sure he put us back on course. He's a great listener and a tireless worker. That was something we had in common.

LIEUTENANT GENERAL MICHAEL T. FLYNN, U.S. ARMY (RETIRED)

I think the bond between President Trump and me formed due to several things. He has a tremendous appetite for information, and I have a deep understanding of the foreign landscape and a deep knowledge of NATO and how NATO operates. I briefed him on NATO operations, budgets, and capabilities. I also walked Trump through the entirety of Southwest and Central Asia, sort of the middle region of the world. I had spoken to him quite a bit about the war in Ukraine at the time. I got really up to speed on China and some of the things that China was doing militarily, economically, psychologically, and economically. At the time, China was really starting to get involved in all kinds of activities. During the Obama administration, the Chinese seemed to be rising and in a dangerous way.

We both recognized that the world was a dangerous place, and the Obama White House had made it more dangerous for America. Trump and I were both driven by the same purpose, and we trusted each other. That's why what we now call the Deep State went after me so relentlessly. First, we "get Flynn," as former deputy FBI director Andrew McCabe put it, and then "we get Trump."

What I didn't know at the time was that the FBI had been investigating me since early 2016, maybe even before that. They didn't officially start their investigation until August 2016, but the evidence shows I was being spied on by the government I'd served—and by a president I'd served, Barack Obama.

There was no way the FBI went rogue with its investigation of me. Since I was the former director of the Defense Intelligence Agency (DIA), an intelligence chief who was read into our nation's most vital secrets, there's no chance President Obama didn't know about the investigation, and in that January 5 meeting, he wanted an update.

We know about the January 5 meeting because of a memo that Obama's outgoing national security advisor, Susan Rice, emailed herself two weeks later, on January 20. It was the day of Trump's inauguration, and the Obama team had only hours left in office when Rice sent the memo to herself. Many people have called this her "CYA" (cover your ass) memo—she was protecting herself and Obama from

22

the possible consequences if the scheme against President Trump was discovered. But it's also possible that Rice left the memo out in public because Obama and his top deputies wanted their troops to know who was calling the shots. It wasn't just a few disgruntled and disgraced former bureaucrats out trying to destroy the forty-fifth president of the United States—no, it was his predecessor, forty-four.

I met with Susan Rice multiple times over the many weeks between the transition from the outgoing administration to the incoming administration. A few meetings were one-on-one; others were with her staff briefing us on the Obama administration's various foreign and domestic policies. There was even a very formal and public transition event called "passing the baton" between administrations. I found Susan Rice to be super smart, an absolute bureaucratic and establishment insider, and someone who deeply despised the fact that we had won. Our transition was like intellectual combat during every single meeting. I tried to be as gracious as possible and found her to be a very cold and dark person. There were things I later learned that she did not share as she turned over the reins of the NSA's position. Some of those had to do with intelligence programs that were the absolute purview of the NSA. Those I would have to dig into myself. As the former head of DIA, I was aware of some and had insight into others.

When it comes to Susan Rice, don't get me wrong: She was smart, but she was also shrewd and calculated and protected her boss's policies right up to the end (and likely then some). Everything we discussed was about how wonderful the Obama administration had done, especially in the foreign policy arena. I knew that I had to get through these transition meetings almost as a form of protocol, but looking back, I think the entire time Rice was calculating how to effect my demise from that office in order to undermine a duly elected president. That is what I mean about shrewd and calculating.

Rice was there on January 5 along with Obama, Vice President Joe Biden, Director of National Intelligence James Clapper, Director of the Central Intelligence Agency John Brennan, FBI Director

James Comey, Deputy Attorney General Sally Yates, and a few other conspirators. They were talking about the FBI investigation that was supposed to have been closed the day before, the investigation they opened on me.

I was one of four people in the Trump circle spied on by the FBI as part of what the bureau opened as an umbrella investigation called Crossfire Hurricane. The investigation on me specifically was called Crossfire Razor. I don't know why they used the name Razor. You'd have to ask them.

The investigation on me didn't find anything, not even an unpaid parking ticket. There was nothing there, so they decided to close it. That was January 4. According to an official closing communication dated that day:

> *CROSSFIRE HURRICANE predicated reporting, the absence of any derogatory information or lead information from these logical sources reduced the number of investigative avenues and techniques to pursue. Per the direction of FBI management, CROSSFIRE RAZOR was not interviewed as part of the case closing procedure.*
>
> *REDACTED. The FBI is closing this investigation. If new information is identified or reported to the FBI regarding the activities of CROSSFIRE RAZOR, the FBI will consider reopening the investigation if warranted.*[1]

But the document hadn't been officially approved yet. On the same day, January 4, Crossfire Hurricane's lead agent and head of the FBI's counterespionage unit, Peter Strzok, learned that the Crossfire Razor investigation was still formally open. He relayed what he called the "serendipitously good" news to another FBI official Lisa

---

1   Federal Bureau of Investigation, "Exhibit 1: Case 1:17-cr-00232-EGS Document 198-2," filed May 7, 2020, p. 5, https://storage.courtlistener.com/recap/gov.uscourts. dcd.191592/gov.uscourts.dcd.191592.198.2_1.pdf

Page, with whom Strzok was having an affair. "Our utter incompetence actually helps us," Strzok told Page. He told the rest of the FBI team working on the investigation to "keep it open for now" at the behest of "the 7th Floor."

The seventh floor of the FBI headquarters at the J. Edgar Hoover Building in Washington, DC, is where the offices of the bureau's leadership are, and the evidence shows that Comey and McCabe and the rest were taking orders too. "Hey, we just got word from the White House," Strzok wrote colleagues. "Keep the Flynn investigation open."

The next day, January 5, Obama was briefed on the intelligence community assessment (ICA) about Russian interference in the 2016 election that he'd ordered to be rushed to completion before his administration ended. Contrary to media reports, the intelligence community's seventeen agencies did not contribute to the ICA, titled "Assessing Russian Activities and Intentions in Recent US Elections." Rather, it was a product dominated by a team of CIA analysts hand-picked by CIA Director John Brennan and included input from three other agencies: the FBI, the Office of the Director of National Intelligence (DNI), and the National Security Agency (NSA). The briefing ICA was conducted [and?] prepared by Brennan, Comey, DNI Director James Clapper, and NSA Director Admiral Michael Rogers, and their agencies.

After that briefing on January 5 in the Oval Office, according to Rice's memo, is when they came around to discussing me and the new administration. "Obama had a brief follow-on conversation," wrote Rice, with Comey, Yates, Biden, and herself also present. Rice wrote in her memo:

> *[President Obama began the conversation by stressing his continued commitment to ensuring that every aspect of this issue is handled by the Intelligence and law enforcement communities "by the book". The President stressed that he is not asking about, initiating, or instructing anything from a law enforcement*

perspective. He reiterated that our law enforcement team needs to proceed as it normally would by the book.

From a national security perspective, however, President Obama said he wants to be sure that, as we engage with the incoming team, we are mindful to ascertain if there is any reason that we cannot share information fully as it relates to Russia.

Director Comey affirmed that he is proceeding "by the book" as it relates to law enforcement. From a national security perspective, Comey said he does have some concerns that incoming NSA Flynn is speaking frequently with Russian Ambassador Kislyak. Comey said that could be an issue as it relates to sharing sensitive information. President Obama asked if Comey was saying that the NSC [National Security Council] should not pass sensitive information related to Russia to Flynn; Comey replied "potentially." He added that he has no indication thus far that Flynn has passed classified information to Kislyak, but he noted that "the level of communication is unusual."[2]

The President asked Comey to inform him if anything changes in the next few weeks that should affect how we share classified information with the incoming team. Comey said he would.][3]

In other words, Obama told the FBI director to spy on the incoming White House, the president-elect, and his new national security advisor. That's how the coup began.

---

2   Email memo from Susan Rice to herself for files documenting instructions from President Obama about how to handle Michael Flynn and Sergei Kislyak phone calls, January 20, 2017, https://www.politico.com/f/?id=00000172-2e48-d57a-ad7b-7e6f97060000.
3   Rice email.

I'll get into more details later on about my phone conversations with Sergei Kislyak, the Russian ambassador to the US at the time, but for now I'll just point to the highly irregular nature of the Obama-led discussion about my conversations with Russia's ambassador. Obama, Biden, and the rest knew what I said to Kislyak—they had the transcripts from every single phone call! There was nothing unusual about my speaking with him. I was the incoming NSA. It was my job to reach out to people like Kislyak and other foreign ambassadors and leaders to introduce myself and begin building a relationship with them on behalf of President Trump. But not only did Obama and Biden convene a meeting with members of the intelligence community to discuss my conversations, they wanted to charge me with a crime for it.

According to Strzok's notes,[4] Biden suggested that I could be charged with violating the Logan Act, an arcane, eighteenth-century statute that prohibits negotiations between unauthorized American citizens and foreign governments having disputes with the United States. It's a law that has never been used successfully and that many believe is unconstitutional. Besides, like I say, it was my job to speak and meet with foreign officials. The whole scenario was ridiculous. One analyst on social media speculated they may have come up with the Logan Act idea from an episode of *The West Wing*, a 1990s TV show with Martin Sheen playing a president much like Bill Clinton. I wouldn't be surprised—many in that administration were living in a dark fantasy land, and over the coming years, they plunged all of our country into their ugly fantasies.

The day after the January 5 Oval Office meeting, I set up a meeting with members of the intelligence community (IC). It was a briefing that the Obama administration wanted to make sure the IC leadership could provide to the incoming team on some important issues. I set the meeting up with Clapper, whom I'd known for some

---

4   "Exhibit 10: Case 1:17-cr-00232-EGS Document 198-11," filed May 7, 2020, p. 1, https://storage.courtlistener.com/recap/gov.uscourts.dcd.191592/gov.uscourts.dcd.191592.198.11.pdf.

time. He called me and said, "Hey, Obama has asked us to come brief an intelligence community assessment to the incoming President and key members of his national security team." And I said, "Well, let's set it up in Trump Tower." I told him that we'd have a room set aside and asked when he could let us know who would attend.

Our team consisted of President-elect Trump, Mike Pompeo, Reince Priebus, staffers, and me. It was a very small group. They gave us a classified briefing. The essence of the briefing had to do with Russian interference in our elections. This information, unbeknownst to us at the time, was to be the prelude of the future dark times America was to face with what has become known as "Russiagate."

During the intelligence briefing, I was curious about the "confidence level" of this information. Others in the room from the Trump team had little knowledge, if any, of the concept of confidence levels that the IC assigns to ICAs.

Given an ICA of this magnitude and importance, I felt it was necessary to ask Admiral Mike Rogers specifically about his confidence. Mike was the main presenter along with DNI Clapper, offering comments throughout, along with Director Brennan, who remained relatively quiet and subdued (traits he is not known for). Mike stated that from his agency's perspective, he gave it a medium confidence assessment, which in "Intel-Speak" means you don't have sufficient information to confirm what you're saying, but there is sufficient information to claim there might be smoke. Clapper jumped on that and stated the overall community assessment was high,[5] something we now know to be false.

I said to Mike, "Explain to President-elect Trump, what the confidence level is that you have in this area." We use low confidence, medium confidence, and high confidence to describe the confidence we have in the sources and methods used to collect a given piece of intelligence. Then I asked him, "What's your confidence?" He said he wasn't at a high confidence level.

---

5   Matt Taibbi, Michael Shellenberger, and Alex Gutentag, "CIA 'Cooked the Intelligence' to Hide That Russia Favored Clinton, Not Trump, in 2016, Sources Say," Public News, February 15, 2024, https://public.substack.com/p/cia-cooked-the-intelligence-to-hide.

Mike is a good friend of mine and a very honest guy. He was honest about how he felt. He said, "I'm about medium." And that's what went into the record. The NSA was the one agency that bucked Brennan, Clapper, and Comey's bogus assessment about the Russians' role in the 2016 election.

Did Moscow try to interfere in our election? Sure, just like they had even before the Cold War. That's Moscow being Moscow. But the ICA made it seem like the Russian President had wanted Trump to win, when we now know the opposite is true—the Russians saw Hillary Clinton as offering far greater continuity. So, Rogers' bucking the fake consensus was a big deal. As most Americans now understand all too well, the bulk of our intelligence collection is through signals intelligence, the collection of electronic data like phone calls, emails, texts, etc. When Rogers said the NSA only had medium confidence, that meant the NSA had no rock-solid signals intelligence to prove the case that Brennan, Clapper, and Comey were determined to make.

Trump took it all in like he normally does with information. He listened, and he appreciated it. I saw the briefing like a lot of other intelligence briefings that I've sat through that have been vastly more threatening than what I just heard. When Rogers said he had medium confidence in the Russia interference assessment, I decided not to pay much attention to it. It was much less important than the fact that Russia was breathing down the neck of our allies in Europe. Another big worry was that over in North Korea, Kim Jong-Un, Little Rocket Man, was firing off missiles. Plus, we were still at war in Afghanistan and Iraq. We were coming into a really rough environment to take over the presidency and under the leadership of a man who wasn't a politician. Trump had a great grasp of foreign policy and what was happening. He hated the idea that we were in these endless wars. And it was a top priority to figure out how to get out of them. So, there were real challenges ahead. That's what was on my mind.

As far as the Russian interference stuff went, we looked at it like, "Okay, got it." Nobody believed this was a major threat to our peace and prosperity. It was just another thing on our to-do list as we got ready to go into the White House.

When the meeting was about to break up, Comey said, "Can I take five extra minutes with you?" Everyone left the room but Trump and Comey. It was Comey briefing the president-elect alone on something we were told was too sensitive for anyone else. Trump obliged. That's when he briefed Trump on what came to be known as the Steele dossier, including ridiculous and salacious allegations against President Trump.

It was a collection of fake memos written by a former British intelligence officer named Christopher Steele. As we would later find out, it was paid for by the Hillary Clinton campaign.[6] It was the centerpiece of a dirty tricks operation to frame her rival and his team, including me, as Russian spies. The real shock was that the FBI had used the dossier as evidence to spy on us in the Trump team, first during the campaign, then during the transition, and even when we came to the White House.[7] Comey had directed the espionage campaign against us, and the entire time Obama, as we later discovered, knew everything his intelligence chiefs were doing. But we didn't find any of that out until much later. By then it was too late to put an end to the madness Obama and his cohorts unleashed on me, on President Trump, and, worse, on the American people. Comey briefed Trump only on the famous, and fake, story about the Russian hookers peeing on a bed. That's what the Russians had on Trump, according to Comey. After the meeting between Trump and Comey, I met with Trump up in his Trump Tower office, and he told me how ridiculous he thought Comey's story was. He was unmoved by the entire presentation, and after all the hoopla, it was back down to busi-

---

6   Marshall Cohen, "FEC Fines Hillary Clinton Campaign and DNC over Trump-Russia Dossier Research," CNN, March 30, 2022, https://www.cnn.com/2022/03/30/politics/clinton-dnc-steele-dossier-fusion-gps/index.html.

7   Samantha Raphelson, "FBI Apologizes to Court for Mishandling Surveillance of Trump Campaign Adviser," NPR, January 11, 2020, https://www.npr.org/2020/01/11/795566486/fbi-apologizes-to-court-for-mishandling-surveillance-of-trump-campaign-adviser.

ness to complete the transition and get into the White House to get the country back on track. That was always Trump's focus.

It was a surreal moment. Trump was in an interesting mood because of what he had just been told. He couldn't believe it. He knew it was all garbage. We all did. What we didn't know was that Comey had been in the White House the day before, where Obama, Biden, and their deputies conspired to brief the president-elect on what they all knew was a lie. The plan was to take me out and get to Trump. We're still living through what Obama started on January 5, 2017.

What you'll find in the following pages is an account explaining how America came to this place, where we're going as a nation, and the likely consequences of not acting in time to preserve what our forefathers built and defended with their lives. It's a story I'm telling for the first time. It's a story about my family and our country, and the role I've played protecting them all my adult life, in the US Army, the intelligence community, the White House, and as a private citizen. You'll find details of well-known events that you haven't read before, like how I was pushed out of the White House by the FBI, Obama assets, and Republican Party establishment insiders.

What you won't find is another "narrative" that bends reality to serve political ends. It's not just another point of view from an interested observer. What follows here is the testament of someone who lived up to his commitments and pledges and paid a high price for it. But along the way, I gathered strength from the adversity. My faith was fortified, and I won friends. Thousands of Americans reached out to me and my family and supported us in ways I couldn't possibly have imagined when I first began my journey through life. I'm telling my story for the record—and for you, to show my gratitude for all you've done and continue to do for our great nation. I am also telling the correct and truthful version for my grandchildren and their future grandchildren. This is a story of such historical consequence, someday they and others may all know the true story of General Michael T. Flynn. May God always bless and protect America.

CHAPTER 2

FAMILY IS MY FOUNDATION

BEGINNINGS

When God made Helen Frances Andrews Flynn, He broke the mold. Sure, we're all different, unique, one of a kind. But G-Fly, as her grandchildren called her, was something else entirely, and that's where the story of my life begins. She was the mother of the nine "Tuckerman Ave." Flynns, my remarkable mom.

She was outspoken, a defender of her family, and had that gut feeling about people that served her well. She was an avid reader and a lifelong learner, and was faithful to God, fearlessly independent, and defiant against wrongdoers, and unafraid to call them out — didn't matter who it was. Tell the truth, no matter the consequences. I'm grateful to have all those qualities of character from her.

I was born on Christmas Eve in 1958 in Fort George G. Meade, Maryland. At my birth, there were already five Flynn children: Helen (Lennie), Bill, Clare, Barbara, and Jack. There was a debate about my first name, as the family story goes—I could have been Thomas—but Mom had the final say, and Michael won. All of us are named after a saint, and I am named after Saint Michael, the Archangel.

When my dad got orders to Fort Meade, we first lived in a regular family unit for enlisted men, four floors stacked on top of each other. But with three of us Flynns born during his Fort Meade tour of duty (Barbara, Jack, and me) and the three older kids (Lennie, Bill, and Clare) already there, the Army moved us into a revamped recreation facility. Our living room was once a regulation-size basketball court. Offices were turned into bedrooms, and we had a makeshift kitchen that was formerly the coffee room for the military men, women, and civilians who once called the Flynn residence their rec center.

That lasted about a year. Then, in 1960 my dad got his orders, and we were off to Germany, a small town in Bavaria called Lenggries. We lived nearby in Bad Tolz in Army housing, which ended up being two side-by-side units on the top floor of a three-story housing building. We'd just leave the front doors open between the units. We had two kitchens, two dining rooms, two living rooms, four bedrooms, and two bathrooms. Everything was the same except reversed, including the furniture, rugs, lamps, and so on. Everything was Army-issued. Above our two units was a wide-open space, the building's attic, which ran the entire length of the facility and was where we'd play ball, hold races, and run around with each other for the next three years.

In the summers, we'd all pack into the little green Renault we owned, tie an old wicker basket to the top of the roof filled with crackers, a large thermos of water, and sandwiches. Dad drove, and Mom sat in the passenger side holding bags filled with bathing suits, blankets, and towels, six kids crammed together in the back seat, and off we'd go to a freshwater lake, the Chiemsee. In winter, we'd ski and ice skate, and every morning, we'd all get dressed and hike to the post church for seven o'clock Mass. These morning church excursions were where my older siblings learned to recite the entire Mass in Latin.

We were there for three years. By the time we left, Mary had been born, and now there were seven kids from about sixteen months to sixteen years old. I was primed for just about anything life had in store with faith, family, and freedom as the bedrock of my life.

Back in the States, Dad was about to make a life change that would affect us all. He was set to retire as a sergeant first class after twenty years in the Army. He had served our country from World War II (at eighteen fresh out of De La Salle Academy in Newport, Rhode Island), through a long deployment during the Korean War, to his last post in Fort Dix, New Jersey. But for Mom, there was no way we were going to New Jersey to live in another Army housing unit. No, the ocean was calling her home to Rhode Island.

My mother's mother, my grandmother "Gam," had passed away while we were in Germany. Mom had traveled back to the US during Gam's final days and returned to Germany just before the day she died. Gam left a small cottage on Tuckerman Avenue in Middletown—a one-bedroom cottage. Dad, Mom, and her brother, Frank Andrews, a World War II Navy captain, had agreed that Mom and all us kids would live in the Middletown house while Dad finished the last five or six months of his military career in New Jersey. I was five at the time.

Tuckerman Avenue was just the right size for one person, maybe two. But with the Flynns, it was home to two adults and seven children, and eventually two more. There was no washing machine, one mini-bathroom with no room for a bathtub, a kitchen with a refrigerator the size of an old-fashioned ice box, no dishwasher, and essentially no heat. It was a beach cottage the size of a postage stamp, with no insulation, that was built on dirt—no foundation just a box with walls.

We had no furniture or household goods to our name. No tables and chairs or kitchenware. We had the clothes on our backs and a few in suitcases when we arrived from Germany, along with whatever my grandmother had left in the kitchen drawers and cupboards for dishes, glasses, and utensils, and a bunch of brown, scratchy Army-issued blankets.

What we did have was the Atlantic Ocean as our backyard. And that was a miracle in my life—the wide-open sea, surf, and rocks to climb on and dive off.

On that day in April 1963 when we arrived at our new quarters on Tuckerman Avenue, the first thing we did was run to the beach and jump in the ocean, clothes and all. That beautiful ocean became our sanctuary, our friend, and our teacher. It's where I learned to surf—the sport that teaches you how to be spiritually alone and at peace, even when the tides and turbulent currents are coming at you.

To this day, all of us love the ocean, no matter the season. Many of my siblings, like myself, are still grabbing a surfboard whenever we can and looking for that wave to ride. I'm known to say it's not the size of the wave that counts; it's how you ride it—my life philosophy in a nutshell.

In the Flynn family, you learned how to swim early. It was my mom's way. One of my very first memories is of my mother putting me into the deep end of a pool and letting go. That's how she taught all the Flynn kids, boys and girls, how to swim. She'd dump you in the water, and then you'd come to the top and start splashing around. She'd do that several times, and eventually, you'd learn how to get to the side of the pool on your own. It's survival. You just start kicking and paddling, and it becomes a natural thing, and then you're swimming.

When I went to the pool as an older brother with my three younger siblings, Mary, Charlie, and Joe, I would help my mother at the poolside. She'd say, "Hand me Joe, Charlie, and Mary." I would hand the kids over to her. And one by one, she'd let them go down under until they swam to the top. It's as if my mother had some inborn sense about knowing what kids can handle and how to push them to do things on their own that seem hard but aren't really. That's one of the things I owe my mother, among lots of other things: learning how to get people to rise to their best. And to this day, whether I'm swimming in a pool or the ocean, or surfing, the water is like a sanctuary for me, and for all the Flynns.

It was great arriving in Rhode Island, the place where both my parents had grown up. As young Army kids, we were used to new environments where families came from all over. Families would come, and they'd go. The first question you'd ask a new Army kid at school was when they were leaving! They'd ask you the same. Rhode Island was different.

We had no idea that Mom had been class valedictorian at Rogers High School or that Dad was captain of his high school football team before leaving for World War II. They were popular in their youth, and now that they were "back" in their old stomping grounds, it was often the case that when people would meet us "Flynns" for the first time, they'd say, "Hey, aren't you one of Charlie and Helen's kids?"

Charles Francis Flynn and Helen Frances Andrews Flynn were born and raised in Newport, Rhode Island. Dad's father was Henry Flynn, a World War I Army veteran; his wife was Katherine Burns. Mom's father was Frank Andrews, a World War I and II torpedo expert; her mother was Helen Fallon. The two Irish families had upwards of eighteen brothers and sisters—my great aunts and uncles—all living in Newport's Irish Fifth Ward. Over the years, I learned that there was rarely a family with an Irish surname that wasn't related to me somehow—cousins were everywhere in Newport. This experience was new to me. As a military kid, being around relatives is not common. My brother Joe is the keeper of our family's genealogy: of who was who, who married whom, and how we are all related. It was a big transition for our family when my parents decided to move back to their home base.

From Fort Meade, Maryland, in the "basketball court" house, to Bad Tolz, Germany, in the two-unit military housing setup, to Middletown, Rhode Island, in the little cottage by the sea, all in six years. That was my life for that formative time, with six brothers and sisters, and two more to come over the next few years, Charlie and Joe.

Nine kids. Back then a family that size wasn't all that exceptional. It wasn't exactly the norm either, but plenty of Catholic families had ten, eleven, twelve kids. My wife, Lori, comes from a Portuguese family with seven children.

What's it like being part of a big family? I remember as kids we went through lots of milk, maybe ten gallons a week. You make ends meet. We ate a lot of peanut butter and jelly sandwiches.

Sometimes we'd have to split a sandwich in two because there wasn't enough bread. So, you cut your peanut butter and jelly sandwich in half and pass it to the next Flynn kid in line, and that's your school lunch. Sacrifice becomes part of your regular routine. But you don't think of it as a sacrifice because you're sharing what you have with people you love—your brothers and sisters.

There was no question that Tuckerman Avenue needed repairs if it was to be our family's landing from the military, so Mom set her sights on making the meager space livable, enrolling us in school, and finding a carpenter willing to figure out how to put an addition onto the house that had very little land to begin with.

That's when Frank Flowers came into the picture. He was a great carpenter and easygoing enough to deal with seven raucous kids running around while he pounded nails, put up walls, and placed down floorboards. He saved that little cottage from collapsing around us. He fixed the walls, put some cabinets in the kitchen, and added two small bedrooms and an open deck. He had to remove the original front door, close it up to build a wall, and then construct an open living area that looked more like a wide corridor in an office building. That change meant the only way into the one-door cottage for a few months was to climb in through a window. So we did.

No matter, a house with no door was no problem—not when the ocean was still a stone's throw away. Some years later, Mom would name the house "Sea Lodge." She even had a fancy sign made during her time selling real estate. That was after she earned her undergraduate degree (one course at a time over years) and later a law degree at sixty-three years old, all while raising nine kids. Sea Lodge was the perfect name for that home. It had true meaning for us as we grew up, left, came back for visits, stayed for longer periods with our own families over the years, or when friends and relatives needed a place to stay for a few days, for one reason or another.

SCHOOL DAYS

Whenever Mom could enroll her kids in a Catholic school while my father was in the military, she did. It was the same when we settled into Sea Lodge.

St. Mary's School, attached to the historic St. Mary's Church in Newport, is where I went to primary school. It was about two miles from Sea Lodge: a walk along the shoreline of First Beach, up the famous Cliff Walk at the surfers' end of the beach, then straight up Memorial Boulevard, onto Bellevue Avenue, and down Friendship

Street to St. Mary's School. Most mornings, we'd all pile into the Renault, shipped from overseas, and Dad, who was now working as a teller in a bank in Newport, would drop five kids off at St. Mary's. My older sister, Lennie, went to St. Catherine Academy for Girls, which was about half a mile away.

Clare would pack one lunch bag with either saltines and peanut butter or peanut butter and jelly sandwiches. Having your own brown lunch bag to carry, or better yet—a lunchbox—was an expense not in the budget for the Flynn kids. So, at lunchtime, Clare would go from classroom to classroom and hand out wax paper–wrapped lunches one by one to each of us.

Most days, we'd walk the two miles home, climb in the window door, bother Mr. Flowers as he finished whatever carpentry he was tackling that day, head to the beach from the backyard, eat whatever was offered for dinner, claim a cot, grab a blanket, and do it all again the next day. As poor as we were during those early days, I never really noticed it. It was all normal for me. We always had each other, a PB&J, a glass of milk, and, of course, the ocean as our playground.

FAMILY TRAGEDY

I was nine when my parents got the call every parent dreads. Lennie, their eldest child, was in the Rhode Island Hospital after the car she was driving was struck head-on by a Providence Fire Department firetruck. Lennie was a freshman at Rhode Island College (RIC) in North Providence and on her way home when the accident occurred. Her fiancé, Charlie Dwyer, was with her. He was from Newport, a Marine Corps vet who had served in the Vietnam War and had joined the Middletown Police Department. He had driven to pick up Lennie from college, and the two of them were heading home to Middletown when the accident happened on February 27, 1968, just days before her twenty-first birthday on March 2. Lennie was driving the car.

For the next six months, she was in a coma. She never woke. Lennie was a beautiful woman with a bright, light smile. One of my great memories is of her cooking Jiffy Pop popcorn on the top of the stove in that tiny kitchen. Popcorn was a staple in our house because it was cheap. You could throw it into a frying pan, throw a stick of butter in, and you're good to go. That's one of my favorite memories of her, taking care of all her younger brothers and sisters and fixing us a treat.

While Mom and Dad went through the trauma of watching their first child slip away in a hospital bed in Providence, traveling back and forth day and night to be by her side and praying for her to live, my sister, Clare, took over caring for the rest of us. She was sixteen years old, a junior in high school, and until August 25, the day Lennie passed on, Clare was in charge much of the time.

She says she liked being in charge, but it forced her to take on adult responsibilities very quickly. We used to kid her and called her "Half-a-Cup Clare." "Why's that?" she asked. Because she only gave us half a cup of milk or juice because she didn't want us to spill it and make a mess.

As sad as this tragedy was for all us kids, our parents were devastated. Joe and Charlie were toddlers at the time; the rest of us were under twelve—Mary, me, Jack, and Barbara. We needed to pull together for Mom and Dad, and by the grace of God, we did.

THE TROUBLE I CAUSED—LORI TO MY RESCUE

I went through a little bit of a wild streak as a teenager and hung around with some kids who were troublemakers. As Joe puts it, I was testing, pushing boundaries, like a lot of kids do. I was fearless as a kid. I'd always look for the biggest hill to skateboard, or surf during a hurricane gale, or the highest cliff to dive off. I was always looking for the next challenge. It also made me alert to danger.

When I was thirteen years old, I was out with a friend and saw a car starting to roll down a hill, heading right for where two children were playing. There was another child in the car, and he'd released the emergency break. The car was rolling quickly toward the two toddlers. I yelled to my friend to grab one of them, and I managed to move the other one out of harm's way. The elders of Middletown recognized my efforts and put my photo in the local newspaper. Having your picture in the paper for a job well done was a big deal for me back then.

Fast-forward to the last eight years of my life, or since 2016, after millions of pictures of me have been published in newspapers from around the world, all of which were attached to articles laced with lies about me. I could have done without all of them.

But as I mentioned, I was no angel as a kid. To my parents' disappointment, I ended up on probation as a teen. I was moving in the wrong direction and hanging out with the wrong crowd. The probation officer would come to our house, and I'd have to answer his questions. Mom sat me down. and I'd have to tell the probation officer about school and what I was doing to stay out of trouble. My brothers and sisters would mill around, pulling faces and trying to hear what the officer had to say.

I straightened myself out after I learned what probation was all about. As it turned out, I was a pretty good athlete and loved to compete, so instead of wasting my energy getting into trouble, I started putting it into playing sports during high school and working as a lifeguard at Second Beach in Middletown during the summers. First Beach was steps away from Sea Lodge, and Second Beach was around the bend of Tuckerman Avenue—an easy walk or run to work during the summer months. In fact, Bill, Barbara, Charlie, Joe, and I were all lifeguards over about six or seven summers, and some of us worked together through those years.

My sister Clare says she always remembers watching one of my football games with our dad. I was maybe sixteen or seventeen. It was the kickoff, and as the whistle blew to start the game, I've got my arm raised, with my finger pointing to the sky and screaming, "CHARGE!" Whenever I was promoted or commended during my military career, my father would remind Clare about that kickoff and my determination to lead and win. We ended up as state high school football champions that year.

THE ROCK OF MY LIFE

God has blessed me in so many ways, but maybe most of all when He brought Lori Andrade into my life as a teenager. I fell in love with my beautiful wife, Lori, when we were just teens. Lori is my rock. She's the steady hand that I needed the day I met her in the late 1970s, and my anchor ever since.

My brothers and sisters agree that it was Lori who really turned me around. I was a rambunctious teenager, but I was smart enough not to blow opportunities, especially this one. I was falling in love.

The first time Lori and I met was the summer before we entered high school. We went steady for two weeks, and then, for whatever reason, we went our separate ways. We'd see each other in the hallways at school but didn't get back together again until our senior year. We'll never forget the exact date, September 18, 1976, because we've been together ever since. Sometimes, our dates were long walks or bike rides. From very early on, I realized this was the person I wanted to spend my life with. It was truly God who put us together and watched over our relationship as it grew.

Lori gave me focus. So did her parents. You can disappoint your own mother and father, or make them mad, but you're still their kid. But if you let down the parents of the girl you like, they'll slam the door right in your face. And they're right to do it.

Lori and I come from strong families. Our parents knew and liked each other. Lori's father, George, was a state police officer. And to be honest, I was a little intimidated the first time I met him. He had stepped out of a truck the wrong way, hurt his foot, and was wearing this big boot and wasn't happy about it. He was in a pretty bad mood, but we got along great. He influenced me in ways that shaped my entire life. He encouraged me to get serious about my education, and I took his advice. Lori's mom, Patricia (we call her Saint Pat, and her many grandchildren call her Gammy), is another miracle in my life. Between those two, they helped guide me, along with my parents, to do better in school and in sports. I was captain of our state champion football team and student body president. George and Pat Andrade were great influences on me.

On our wedding day, May 9, 1981, the priest who married us was a cousin of mine, Father Phillip, a son of my mother's brother Frank and a big part of our family life. During the wedding ceremony, he talked about a part of the beach where we'd go to surf. Surfers called it the Rock. He talked about our marriage and described Lori as the Rock—steady, stable, strong, and unmovable. He said I was like the tide, ebbing and flowing. He knew that I was getting ready to go into the military. And he knew that as a kid, there was a time when I was on the wild side. He knew my nature, and he knew what the two of us needed to thrive as a couple. Father Phillip described me as someone who was always going to ebb and flow like the ocean, while Lori was always going to be strong and unmovable, the landmark by which the marriage kept its compass. Forty-three years later, there's no better description of our marriage than what Father Phillip said on our wedding day. Lori is the Rock.

After our short honeymoon in the Bahamas, I was commissioned into the Army and was assigned to Fort Bragg, North Carolina. It was the first time as adults that either of us had ever lived anywhere but Middletown. With our whole life together in front of us, we couldn't have been more excited.

CHAPTER 3

SOLDIER, LEADER, HUSBAND, FATHER

EARLY ARMY YEARS

I almost wasn't a soldier. That's hard for me to imagine now, given how much of my life was in the Army and how much I owe to what I consider America's greatest institution. But my plan had been to join a different service branch—the Marine Corps. And that all changed with one unexpected meeting in the summer of 1978.

I'd just finished my freshman year at the University of Rhode Island, and I was working as a lifeguard at the beach when one afternoon my father told me, "Hey, when you get off work today, come home." I remember thinking, *Man, I'm in trouble for something.* Once I got home, there was my father and an Army major sitting at the kitchen table. My first thought was that I was in worse trouble than I'd imagined.

In fact, it was another great moment in my life, a blessing that would shape my future, like meeting Lori. The major said he had an ROTC scholarship available, and I asked what I needed to do to get it. I played a lot of intramural sports during my freshman year and swam for the URI swim team. I also played collegiate water polo, a water sport I excelled at (eventually making Division-1 All-New England). However, during my freshman year, I wasn't going to class that much. Let's just say, I wasn't much of a sit-down student. I lived in the ROTC department at the campus gym and played a lot of basketball. That's where I met this Army major who took a liking to me. The major told me I had to get my grades up, and I said I would. He also told me, "Don't worry about the Marines." The next day I drove over to the university, did the paperwork, and was offered a full ROTC scholarship.

All my instructors were Vietnam vets. The war had just ended a few years before, and a lot of people were wary of the military. Some people were outright hostile to the military and the men and women who'd served their country in uniform. My instructors were serious and impressive men. They deserved not just the respect but also the admiration of their fellow Americans. I sure looked up to them. I said I wanted to enter the infantry, but my professor of military science (Lieutenant Colonel O'Grady), a special forces officer with Vietnam experience, sat me down one day and said, I know you'd do well in the combat arms, but intelligence is where you need to go, and specifically this relatively new field of electronic warfare that was emerging with advanced technologies (this was the early eighties!). I gave it a shot on my military branch assignment requests and got in. I was assigned to the 82nd Airborne Division, based at Fort Bragg, now Fort Liberty, North Carolina.

The 82nd is a famous, heralded military organization with a great history. Talk about service and sacrifice. It was first constituted as an infantry division in 1917, during World War I. It drew soldiers from all forty-eight states, which is how it got the nickname "All-American." That's what the "AA" shoulder patch on our uniform stands for.

The 82nd fought on the Western Front in World War I, and for World War II it was reorganized as the Army's first airborne division. Its paratroopers jumped into Sicily, Salerno, and then in the early morning of June 6, 1944, Normandy. The division faced a month of relentless combat in France that summer with heavy casualties. According to commanding officer Major General Ridgway's post-battle report, the 82nd saw "33 days of action without relief, without replacements. Every mission accomplished. No ground gained was ever relinquished." That August, they made the fourth and final combat jump of the war, Market Garden. I couldn't have been prouder to become a part of that great history.

I held a variety of assignments with the 82nd Airborne Division, first as a second lieutenant and platoon leader. During those formative years, I had deployments to Panama, Honduras, and other parts of Central America. In those days we were fighting the Sandinistas and Somozans in Nicaragua, and all manner of other insurgents in Central and South America. The Soviet Union and the Cold War were still our nation's main enemy, and the proxy wars raged all around us. One of those proxy wars was being played out in 1983 on a little tiny island called Grenada (the Isle of Spice).

Grenada was the United States' first foreign engagement since Vietnam, and President Ronald Reagan was determined to show our adversaries that Americans had what it took to defeat communist forces, especially in our own sphere of interest.

Grenada is a small island nation in the eastern Caribbean, one hundred miles north of Venezuela. Its government was under communist leadership, and after an internal coup threatened to destabilize other nations in the region, including US allies, the Organization of Eastern Caribbean States filed a formal request for help with the White House. President Reagan sent more than 7,000 troops for a conflict that lasted from October 25 to 29. Nineteen American troops lost their lives, and hundreds were wounded during the course of Operation Urgent Fury. We fought Grenadian forces as well as Soviet and Cuban troops and stayed on for several months to help stabilize the situation.

I was 1st Platoon leader, Alpha Company, 313th Military Intelligence Battalion, 82nd Airborne Division. 1st Platoon was a signals-intelligence-collection and electronic warfare–jamming platoon. For the time, it was a pretty sophisticated outfit.

Once you enter the service and you begin to realize that this is where you fit, this is what you're good at, it's a special feeling. It's a calling. You feel good about that kind of leadership role. And as a young officer leading a platoon, you're responsible for the lives of twenty-five to forty people, mostly people even younger than yourself.

What a lot of those young people don't fully understand when they enlist is they've signed up to potentially give their lives for this country. Most people don't understand that at first. Not young kids. The recruiters don't tell them, but that's really what this is about. You realize it only as you train with your unit, especially a combat unit preparing to deploy to a war zone. Then you begin to realize, this is real. There's going to be somebody on the other side of that hill who wants to kill you.

Once we landed in Grenada, we had a few tasks: oust the Cubans, help the government, push communist influence out of the Caribbean, and save the American medical students who were being held against their will.

Many of those in my collection and jamming platoon were exceptional Spanish-speaking electronic warfare/signals collection analysts and linguists. Many were from Puerto Rico, some from Los Angeles, and a couple from New York City. All were tough paratroopers whom you did not want fighting against you—we were well trained and always ready for a fight—that was the 82nd Airborne way, and still is.

We were getting briefed on the situation while I walked a group of about ten guys off the back of a C-130 with all our equipment and weapons. As we walked onto the tarmac, there were about a dozen body bags lined up right there.

We didn't get very far when someone at the end of the airfield called out, "Hey, just sit there for a minute." My platoon sergeant and I got a briefing: Two hilltops away, one of our brigades was still engaged with a Cuban unit. In the meantime, my platoon was sitting there with the dead soldiers in body bags lying right next to them. They're staring at the body bags until finally, a detail moved the bodies onto the airplane.

Usually, our fallen warriors are honored with what we call "ramp ceremonies," where the dead are put into steel caskets and moved onto the plane with honors. But we couldn't do that because there was still close fighting not far away. A mortar round could have hit that airfield or hit that plane and killed more of our soldiers.

That memory of my platoon looking on their fallen fellow warriors is burned into my mind and soul. It made me fully aware of the responsibility I had to those under my command. It made me focus on the kids I led, just eighteen or nineteen years old, and that they might be killed. You think to yourself, they are just starting life. They joined the military to serve the country. They married their high school sweethearts and had a child, or maybe some of these kids will never meet their own child.

You know the soldiers who give their lives for the country, and you know their families too. Sometimes you bump into the families later in life. You might get to meet the child your soldier never met, and now the son is fourteen years old and just starting high school. Part of that boy's strength comes from knowing his father gave his life for his country and for the men and women he served with. An awful lot of my strength comes from that, too, knowing what they have given and sacrificed. You never forget the people under your command who have given their lives in service to their country.

In Grenada, one of our missions was to set up listening posts on pieces of high ground. One was at the end of the airfield looking over the water where one day I heard someone yelling that it looked like some guys were drowning. I ran and looked over a forty-foot cliff to see two soldiers out at sea, probably one hundred yards off the coast. They were in a small life raft, which was losing air. I'm watching this unfold, and I'm thinking, *Man, these guys are in trouble. They're going to drown.* I yelled out to my guys, "Hey, call up headquarters. Let them know I'm going to go in after them."

Here's where my experience as a surf rescue lifeguard came into play—and also my daredevil antics as a teenager. I'd jumped off lots of bridges and cliffs in my life, so it wasn't that big a deal. I knew what I was doing. I went to the edge of the cliff and looked down. I saw the waves coming in and going out, and I waited. I wanted to know if there were rocks down there; when I saw it was clear, I waited for the wave to come in and jumped.

The ocean was deep enough. I immediately beelined out to the two soldiers, and I got to them quickly. A good lifeguard knows that you never go right to the drowning man because they'll take you down with them. I swam up to about five feet from them and saw that they were hanging on to the life raft and it was losing air quickly now. I was trying to get them to calm down, but they were tired. I told them I would take one guy at a time. I asked them who was the best swimmer and told him to stay with the raft until I got back.

I took the first guy to the cliff and told him to grab hold of it. I said, "You're going to be okay. Sit on that ledge. Don't move." I went back out and got the other guy, brought him back to the ledge, and got him up on it too.

It was starting to get dark, and by then there's a helicopter and a rescue team on the scene. That was also a dangerous situation. The rescue team came down and brought them up into the helicopter and came back down for me. I asked the rescue team guy, "You don't think I can swim back to the shore?"

"Please come up," he replied. "It's better to come up now." So, they brought me up to the helicopter.

When my commanding officer found me, he was very mad. At first anyway. Eventually, we became very close friends over the years, but he was mad at the time. So were a lot of the brass, and they held it against me for a long time.

I had a couple of black sea urchin needles taken out of my feet, was given some vinegar to reduce the pain, bandaged them up, put my boots back on, walked over to the two soldiers whom I had just help pull out of the ocean, and asked if they were okay. They both thanked me, but the person they probably should have been most grateful to was my mother, Helen Flynn—for tossing all the Flynn kids in the water and teaching us how to swim, and how to be fearless.

EDUCATION OF AN INTELLIGENCE OFFICER

After Grenada, I went on to serve in my first of three training assignments and my second tour at Fort Huachuca, the Army's Intelligence Center. This assignment gave me my first glimpse into future warfare—I was assigned as one of the instructors to teach intelligence in low-intensity conflict and multinational operations. The timeframe was in the middle of the Soviet invasion of Afghanistan, and we were watching their operations closely—learning all we could about how the Russians were being beaten by this very difficult, but what appeared to be a poorly organized, foe in the mujahideen.

I then went on to an assignment in the Pacific—the 25th Infantry Division (Tropic Lightning). This opened up my eyes to the type of enemies we saw across a wide swath of the Asia-Pacific Rim, especially China. During this very formative assignment, I studied the Chinese military as well as much of the history of the various nations across the Pacific Basin. From India to North Korea, there is much to be learned, and those years in the 25th Infantry taught me to respect other cultures and societies, especially their warfighting abilities. China was emerging then as a great power; I knew it, but I didn't feel our nation's leaders saw what was clearly on the horizon. Living in the region and having the responsibility to prepare a US Army infantry division's leadership with updated and reliable intelligence on a daily basis is a big responsibility, and I took it very seriously. These were some of my early and formative, but very important, tactical intelligence training and education assignments.

After a stint at the US Army Command and Staff College, along with my selection to the prestigious School of Advanced Military Studies, I was eventually promoted to major, and in the summer of 1994, I was sent back to Fort Bragg. Things were building up again in the Caribbean on another island, Haiti. This would become Operation Uphold Democracy.

I was the chief of war plans working for the G3, director of operations of the 18th Airborne Corps, working for Colonel Dan K.

McNeill, who eventually went on to be a four-star general. I was lucky enough to work for him three more times in very critical and impactful assignments, later in my career. If there was one officer who had the most impact on my success in the Army, it was General McNeill—bar none. He was respected across the entire joint force and achieved four stars without ever serving in the Pentagon, a testament to his combat leadership and integrity.

The commanding general of the 18th Airborne Corps, at the time, was Lieutenant General Hugh Shelton, who would later become chairman of the Joint Chiefs of Staff. He was a superb commander and leader.

We planned the final parts of the operation to seize Haiti's airfield and subsequently fight the Haitian military, a third-rate group of thugs, as well as some Cubans who were also on the island. It was a real mess, but this was my first real taste of Joint, Multinational and Unconventional Operations at the Joint Task Force Level.

I learned an enormous amount in Haiti, including how to view intelligence while deployed in combat; how to integrate intelligence with operations; how a small insurgent force could hold off a much larger and more organized military simply due to knowing the indigenous, physical terrain; and that the US was not set up to support warfighting. This would later come back to haunt our armed forces in Iraq and Afghanistan, a problem set I was determined to address in a published report, that was both controversial and influential, called *Fixing Intel: A Blueprint for Making Intelligence Relevant in Afghanistan*.

After Haiti, I was assigned to Fort Polk, Louisiana, commonly referred to as "Snake Central" because of the abundance of wildlife. I was going to replace the senior intelligence trainer. Normally, that position went to a lieutenant colonel and former battalion commander, someone with much more experience than I had—I was still a young major. Neither Lori nor I was happy about it at first. We thought we might wind up living out our days at "Snake Central," but the experience turned out to be game-changing for me.

I had the honor and privilege to observe and work alongside some of our very best military leaders, like then-Colonels Stanley McChrystal and David Petraeus, both of whom would later distinguish themselves in Iraq and Afghanistan. You couldn't work alongside such men without developing a passionate commitment to do everything possible to give them everything they needed to win, and from my standpoint, it was evident that intelligence and our intelligence system just weren't giving them what they needed.

The Army was still focused on big tank battles (presumably with the Soviet Red Army, or any enemy that would fight us in a big land battle as in World War II) even after Vietnam, where we'd been badly beaten up by a well-organized network. So, at Fort Polk, there were many late-night discussions about how to fight against guerrilla forces, breaking the connectors that made them an effective network, and then destroying them piece by piece. This was the beginning of the development of a truly effective system to win such wars.

It required much better technology; a greatly increased tempo of activity by our forces; more skilled and operationally savvy intelligence officers, interrogators, and fighters; and a new approach to battle: decentralizing decision-making that put the talents of American soldiers to their maximum effectiveness. The bottom line was that intelligence would be vastly more important. I was there at the origins.

This new approach took formal shape under Stanley McChrystal in Iraq over a decade later. It's what enabled his Task Force 714 to do so well, but it didn't happen quickly, and it really didn't get going until we realized we were losing in Iraq. The pieces were plugged in one at a time. Among the things I brought to the intelligence system for the joint force, and to those commanders rotating through Fort Polk's elite training center, was something rarely used, but it turned out to be super important for the next two decades of warfighting. It was simply called "pattern analysis."

Pattern analysis is a very detailed form of intelligence work that requires the complete breakdown of an enemy's cell structure, much like a doctor would break down a disease to find a cure. As I look back on my two years' training twenty combat brigades, this type of work would eventually pay off when we started fighting al-Qaeda and other terror networks. Also at Fort Polk, I learned how ineffective our human intelligence and interrogation operations were. They were essentially nonexistent and poorly executed, if at all. I resolved to fix it, but it wasn't taken seriously until we got to Iraq.

The fact is that no matter how brilliantly we organized ourselves, no matter how accurate our focus might be, the fundamental requirement for good intelligence is the total commitment to the truth. This may seem obvious, and any sensible American realizes that bad information will automatically lead to bad decisions, bad strategy, and likely defeat. Yet some of our most famous intelligence officers, military and civilian alike, have found ways to rationalize the production of seriously misleading information for our policymakers.

It's hard to say exactly when it started, but one of the most important accounts is in a book about intelligence and the Vietnam War, *War of Numbers*, written by a CIA analyst suitably named Samuel Adams.

Adams carefully studied our intelligence on the Vietcong and found that if the numbers were correct, there were very few of them left since the number of deaths and desertions greatly exceeded the level of recruitment. But this was obviously false, and Adams tried to expose the lies for the better part of ten years, all to no avail. CIA and the military had their numbers—numbers that showed we were winning the war—and would not change them.

Adams was right, but the official numbers were endorsed over and over. How could this be?

Part of the answer is that the intelligence community kept quiet when the civilian and military leadership was making false claims about America's war effort: like the Vietcong was shrinking, and America was winning. When Adams and others presented more accurate data, showing the enemy was much stronger than we admitted, it was dismissed.

We call this politicizing intelligence, when what we really mean is that leadership doesn't want to hear bad news, so if you want to keep your job, best not be the bearer of it. So, you just keep quiet. But that wasn't my way, and as the political leadership found out when I was director of the DIA—I told the truth.

But there's something even worse that happened along the way, whether it started with Vietnam or before: Our government not only incentivized lying, which is bad enough, it created a culture in which the people who rose to the top succeeded by lies. As we would find out with Russiagate, they'd lie about anything, even if it poisoned the country.

LEARNING TO LEAD

In the summer of 1997, I was named to lead a battalion in the 82nd Airborne Division as a lieutenant colonel, and my father came to the ceremony at Fort Bragg. He was seated in the front row underneath the tent and right next to him sat the 18th Airborne Corps commander. My father turned to the general and said, "This is the first time I've sat underneath one of these tents that I didn't have to put up." The general laughed. My father the retired sergeant was very proud that his son the lieutenant colonel had just taken command of the 313th Military Intelligence Battalion. It has a great legacy and history of great men and women who have served in it.

About two weeks into my command, a noncommissioned officer (NCO) approached me to say that a helicopter had gone down at a training area near Mott Lake. "What do we know?" I asked.

"We think everybody on it died," he said. This terrible tragedy helped me learn how to lead by staying steady.

I told him to get my driver, a kid named Scotty Gillem. I'll never forget him. Scotty drives up, and I told him to make sure that the radio from headquarters was there. I wanted to make sure we had good communications because that's essential when something goes wrong, especially when tragedy hits and men have died.

I'm the new battalion commander, in charge of about 600 people, and everyone is watching me because, as I learned as a young officer, soldiers' responses are keyed to the responses of the man or woman in charge. When I watched senior officers I admired handling difficult situations, I learned that one important quality, if not the most important, is a steady demeanor. There will always be crises, especially in the military. We use dangerous instruments, many of them designed to kill, so it's important to show that you're steady.

It was a forty-minute drive to the training area where the helicopter had gone down. As soon as I got to the tree line, I could see the smoke. It was about an hour or so after the helicopter crashed. We got out of the vehicle and then walked up this dirt road, probably one hundred yards into the tree line, and walked right up to the crash site. There was a large black patch on the ground the size and shape of a helicopter. It was all burned up with a bunch of small bumps, no more than two feet high. Those were the bodies. I remember the smell of the burning fuel, and the bodies too.

Most of the soldiers who'd died on the helicopter were mine. They were from the intelligence battalion taking photos from the helicopter, doing what we call imagery collection. They were out there preparing for a big training exercise. The helicopter had made a banking move but didn't make the tree line and went down.

As a commander, you're responsible for the lives of all your soldiers, all the men and women in your command. Along with the Aviation Brigade commander, I spent hours ensuring that the site was secured because there was going to be an investigation to find out what happened. In the military, we go through all sorts of protocols to prevent mishaps and tragedies, and when one happens, we want to ensure it doesn't happen again. The other part of my task that day was just as important: to talk to the unit—men and women who'd lost their friends and fellow warriors—and I eventually spoke to each one of the families to tell them that their loved ones had died. I had to be steady for the sake of the battalion, and for the fallen, their comrades in arms, and their families. I was grateful that senior officers I admired as great leaders reached out to me and gave me guidance, and I tried to pass on that wisdom to younger officers.

I'm not great at hearing myself praised, even if it's something true and not just someone trying to flatter me. But there is one compliment I don't mind hearing: that I treat the people working with me well. This I owe to my father. He always told us to treat others the way we would like to be treated. That helped me rise as a young officer. But it's not like you're one of the boys. No, you're their leader. You're making decisions about their lives. You're trying to maximize their potential.

I was always trying to maximize my soldiers' potential. I wanted them to discover what they could do, because if they learned what their potential was, it could save them. When a soldier screwed up badly, I'd bring them in and drill them. They didn't like it. It was scary for them—as a company commander, I could take their rank. One year I hit on an idea of how to get through to them, so I'd go through a series of questions. I'd ask, are your parents still alive and together? Which of your parents do you talk to the most? When was the last time you spoke to your mom? Do you still love your mom? And I had their mom already on the phone. And I'd give the phone to the soldier, and I'd sit there and listen. Some of the mothers would rant and rave, and some would cry. It got out that I would make the soldiers call their moms, but I saved kids by having them talk to their moms, and eventually, the soldiers thanked me for making them talk to their mothers. To top it off, that year, I had the highest graduation rate and the lowest discipline rate of our two training brigades.

I knew that family is the foundation of everything—the foundation of our communities and country, as well as a person's well-being. Even as we moved across the country, from assignment to assignment, Lori was the Rock. Just as Father Phillip had said on our wedding day.

Lori says she loved being an Army wife, but I know it wasn't always easy. When I was deployed abroad, she took on the day-to-day affairs of running a family that are usually split between husband and wife, like managing the household budget and bills; getting our two sons, Michael and Matthew, off to various sports and other school functions; and making sure college applications got turned in on time.

But there was such great support from our community. The soldiers' wives took care of each other, just as their husbands looked after each other on the fields of battle. We lived all around the country—including Massachusetts, Louisiana, Hawaii, Arizona, Kansas, Florida, Virginia, and Washington, DC, among others. That was a big education for two people who grew up in a small town in southern New England. And we were always returning to Fort Bragg, North Carolina, home to the 82nd Airborne Division. My son Michael always tells people that Fort Bragg is like his second home because we were based there so often. It's where he had lots of his most memorable childhood experiences, playing golf, baseball, and basketball.

It wasn't always easy on him and Matthew, but they took to it like it was an adventure. When kids used to ask Michael how he could move around every two or three years, he would say to them, "I don't know how you can live in one place for your whole life."

Our moving around the country took on a rhythm of its own, like the ebb and flow that Father Phillip talked about. But the music changed with the terrorist attacks on September 11, 2001. My career went into a different phase, and so did our country, for better and worse.

CHAPTER 4

FIXING INTELLIGENCE

GLOBAL WAR ON TERROR BEGINS

I was at Fort Bragg when the planes hit on September 11, 2001. I was the chief of intelligence for the entire 18th Airborne Corps. We had been involved in heavy planning for operations in the Balkans (another conflict zone that taught me many things about multinational operations). When the planes hit the Twin Towers in New York City, my sergeant major (Heber Felix) came into my office, turned on the television, and said, "You've got to see this." Like most Americans, we had no idea what was really happening, then the plane hit the Pentagon, and then news of the plane going down in the now famous field in Pennsylvania came across the wires.

At Fort Bragg, we immediately knew the nation was under attack. The phones started to ring off the hook. My boss received a call from the national military command center in the Pentagon to place the entire corps on alert and our corps staff assembled with the commanding general. From that point on, our entire warfighting focus turned to the wars we didn't know then but that we would be fighting for the next two decades. With new guidance now coming in from Washington, DC, we immediately started planning for an invasion of Afghanistan, a place that would forever change my life.

Since June 2001, I'd been serving as the assistant chief of staff, G2, 18th Airborne Corps North Carolina. The job was to provide intelligence support to nearly 150,000 combat and combat support forces, including the famed 82nd Airborne Division, the 101st Airborne Division (Air Assault), the 10th Mountain Division, and the 24th Mechanized Infantry Division, as well as many other formidable combat forces filling the ranks of this Airborne Corps. It was a big responsibility that I felt very well prepared for despite the challenges we were about to face.

Fort Bragg, by that point, was our second home, as my son Michael puts it. It was where my military career started and where it was grounded. I served at Fort Bragg from the rank of second lieutenant to brigadier general and all ranks in between. And with the scope and scale of the Global War on Terror ramping up after the attacks on September 11, Bragg once again became the center of the universe.

The 18th Airborne Corps was designated Combined Joint Task Force (CJTF) 180, and I was redesignated as its senior intelligence officer. We deployed into Afghanistan in early 2002 along with a combined joint task force of principally NATO nations. This force grew to nearly forty-six nations in the subsequent decades of this war, but this early deployment, we found an environment that was disorganized, out of reach for most normal force deployments we had previously experienced, and without any true national objectives. It was a scene of total chaos.

Given the early confusion about objectives and policy, I recall one conversation with a very senior general who flew in from Washington, DC. We were standing on an Afghan dirt road we called "Disney Drive," along a then wide-open Bagram Airbase, when he told us not to start building up forces or anything permanent here, that we didn't plan on being here very long, and we needed to do the job and get out immediately. A couple of us looked at each other and thought, *What planet is this guy from?*

That first deployment to Afghanistan for me lasted approximately five months, then I was off to another assignment. I eventually spent over three years of my life in Afghanistan. That said, given the scale of the initial alliance and the deployment, people were wondering from the very start how long we were going to be there. I could see the [bureaucratic?] machinery start to kick in early on, and I thought, *We'll be here forever*.

I remember giving a briefing on the ground in Afghanistan that summer, and an officer asked, "What's the size of the enemy we face?" I'm someone who, if asked an honest question, will give you an honest answer. I pointed to a map and said there are about 500,000 over the border in Pakistan. I could tell by the look on his face that this wasn't information he was ready to hear, never mind process—half a million? But it was true. The scope of our war was enormous, and few from the leadership, civilian or military, understood what that meant.

The more you advance up the ranks in our military, the more time you spend with senior military officers and political officials. In conversations with high-level officials during wartime, you have an obligation to speak up if you don't think something is going right. You have a responsibility to the men and women who rely on you to protect their lives to tell the truth, and I will always tell the truth.

Unfortunately, that's not always the case with all our great nation's senior officials. One of the most destructive lies was when Colin Powell sat at the United Nations on February 5, 2003, with CIA director George Tenet sitting right behind him, and claimed that Saddam Hussein still possessed weapons of mass destruction. Powell later acknowledged that it was a massive intelligence failure.

Later on, Powell criticized me. He speculated on the reasons for my departure from my post as DIA director. It was in private emails that weren't meant to be seen publicly, but they'd been hacked and leaked, which of course is illegal and shows how our public and private spaces are being corrupted. My point is that, as I said when his hacked emails came out, if Powell wants to call me a jerk, that's okay by me. I know the truth and what I believe in. I think Powell let himself be used. He was secretary of state. He was a four-star general and knew what it meant to send men to war, but it seems he didn't ask really tough questions of the CIA when lives were on the line. It was as much a failure of his leadership as it was an intelligence failure.

It might surprise most Americans, but at the very senior level, there is a lack of attention to detail, and that stacks up. You can feel it all the way down the chain of command. It's like a game of telephone, where the message gets jumbled by the time you get to the end. But in this case, it's much worse when the message is scrambled at the very beginning and by the very people who are making executive decisions.

Generally speaking, that was the core problem with Iraq—it started with false information that was accepted as truth because of a failure to attend to the details. When you're on the ground in the middle of a warzone and people's lives are at stake, the last thing you can afford is to ignore the details. That's what officers are supposed to excel in, attention to detail and judgment. And if the system works the way it's supposed to, the higher up you go, the people at the top have the most experience paying attention to detail, which leads to good decisions.

That was not what happened with Iraq. It started with a massive intelligence failure—Powell was right on that front—the biggest one we've had in this century, and with that, the Bush administration committed us to a war we didn't need to fight.

Although we were in Afghanistan first and initially "won," Iraq became the main effort—the priority. Once that happened, we lost sight of what we needed to do in Afghanistan, despite the great commanders and soldiers we were sending into that theater of war, and Iraq quickly came to consume everything. Practically all resources were diverted to fight an enemy that had nothing to do with the attacks on 9/11.

And our enemy was not a foreign army in the conventional sense of warfighting. This was a guerrilla war. The enemy was an extensive network of combatants out to kill us. We were up against a checkerboard of Iraqis, foreign fighters from Arab countries, enlisting local tribes, and Iranian killers and intelligence operatives who were providing the training, funding, and weapons to their friends in Iraq. We were unprepared for this revolutionary battle.

Our commanders and soldiers needed to know, in granular detail, who we were up against. They needed a clear understanding of the mash-up enemies' interaction. Were we fighting the remnants of Saddam Hussein's Baathist state? Or was this a national uprising against us—an alien occupying force? Were there national leaders, or were there so many tribal, ethnic, religious, and regional divisions within the country that we needed very different tactics to establish order?

In traditional warfare, armies determine the winner and loser of battlefield conflict. One side wins, and the other side surrenders. There is a victor and a vanquished. Not so in a guerrilla war where counterintuitively, the better you do—the more enemies you kill and capture—the worse things can get. Just look at the Soviets in Afghanistan. They killed countless Afghan and foreign jihadis. When it was over, there were more enemy fighters than before. Why? The jihadis say that if we kill one of them, ten new fighters rush to fill the void.

Our political leaders took advantage of the raw emotions that Americans still felt after 9/11—anger, fear, and the desire for revenge—and they leveraged those to maneuver us into a war we didn't need. There was no need to go into Iraq. We were already engaged in Afghanistan, so with Iraq we stretched ourselves thin. Besides, we had had Saddam Hussein boxed in for a decade since Operation Desert Storm by flying all kinds of operations in northern and southern Iraq, and we had economic sanctions on Saddam's regime. Why did we need to muster hundreds of thousands of troops to attack Iraq? It's hard not to think that the Bush administration already wanted to go into Iraq and only wanted a pretext for it.

I'm a student of history, especially military history, like many warriors. It's important to know the causes that led to wars, how the battles unfolded, the character of the historical personalities who made the life-and-death decisions, and the choices that led to victory or defeat. So I see Iraq in the context of how America got into Vietnam. The casus belli was a North Vietnamese attack on a US Navy ship in a northwestern part of the South China Sea known as the Gulf of Tonkin on August 4, 1964.

But there never was any attack on August 4. The Lyndon Johnson administration made it up to take America to war, and three days later, the Senate and House passed the Gulf of Tonkin Resolution, which led to a major escalation and the deployment of US combat troops the next year. It was only forty years later, in 2003, that Johnson's defense secretary, Robert McNamara, publicly acknowledged that the attack never happened.

That lie walked us into a tragedy. Nearly 60,000 Americans, mostly young men, died in Vietnam and hundreds of thousands more were maimed, yet the supposed cause of that war was an attack that never happened. So what about Iraq? The rationale for sending Americans to war in Iraq was a WMD program that didn't exist.

Iraq was a disaster, like Vietnam was a disaster. I feel bad saying so because so many American lives were lost and so many sacrifices made by good young men and women. I don't want those sacrifices to have been made in vain, and in the bigger picture, they weren't. These were Americans, our best and bravest, who gave their lives to defend their nation, protect their fellow countrymen, and keep the faith with the warfighters they stood alongside. But the fact is, we didn't win in Iraq. I saw it first-hand.

INTERROGATING THE ENEMY

In July 2004, once again back at Fort Bragg, I was named director of intelligence for Joint Special Operations Command (JSOC), ▮▮▮▮▮

▮▮▮▮▮▮▮▮▮▮▮▮▮▮▮▮▮▮▮▮▮▮▮▮▮▮▮▮▮▮▮▮▮

▮▮▮▮▮▮. This was another formidable and formative assignment. I was still a full-bird colonel and learned that I was to be promoted to brigadier general. A lot of family came down to Fort Bragg for the ceremony, maybe twenty Flynn family members. It was General Stanley McChrystal, then commanding general of the Joint Special Operations Command, who appointed me. We wound up working together for nearly a decade.

Then Major General Stanley McChrystal, an officer I had worked with previously in the 18th Airborne Corps when he was chief of staff under Lieutenant General Dan McNeill, told me that we needed to fix what was wrong with ████████ missions in Iraq and Afghanistan. I had actually deployed for a few weeks during the month of April 2004 to Afghanistan and Iraq for a visit with McChrystal and ███████. I saw firsthand then how ugly the war was going and how still chaotic the environment was, especially the relationship between conventional and special forces. The unnecessary wasting of time and resources was preventing us from accomplishing what should have been hand-in-glove operations between friendly forces.

Hadn't we learned anything from Vietnam and over many other years of the endless wars America found itself immersed in? It was apparent we had not, and if things didn't improve, we were going to lose this war. One fine point to address during this short assessment trip in April 2004 was the Abu Ghraib scandal, which indicated two things: first, we'd lost focus and discipline; and second, neither the press, the opposition party, nor our enemies were willing to forgive us for it.

This horrific period of US military history would play a lasting role in the war on terror as well as the recruiting of enemy forces for many years to come. In July 2004, I was stepping into a witch's cauldron with every mind to figure out innovative ways to solve some seriously complex problems. Thank God, the talents and capabilities of the commanders, and the men and women of ███████, were up to the task.

There were clearly structural problems and systemic problems. The former we couldn't solve because those decisions were made by political officials. For instance, I remember the first time I went from our headquarters for the multinational forces in Iraq down to Baghdad to brief a senior commander whose headquarters was in one of Saddam's palaces. We decided to grab some chow and were directed to the mess hall, which was an enormous facility the size of a warehouse.

Here we were in the middle of a combat zone in Iraq in a dining facility where you could have anything you wanted. Domino's delivered pizza to the base. Sounds great, right? Just like home. Except in the middle of a war zone, someone has to protect all those shipments of frozen pizzas along all those very dangerous routes. The food companies couldn't fly it in. It had to be brought in on ships to a port in Kuwait, then put on a truck to Baghdad, and then somebody's got to secure that truck along the route. We had a force to secure pizza. I thought to myself, *This is nuts.*

But those decisions weren't in my power to control. I was focused on my job, which meant: one, understanding the enemy; and two, fixing our system of collecting intelligence, which would help us better understand and destroy our enemy.

Interrogating captured fighters was a big part of the job. Any intelligence officer who says he's inside the head of the enemy is lying if he isn't either dealing directly with a former enemy who's come over to our side or talking directly to them and discovering what makes them tick.

This was so important that I couldn't just delegate the task. I personally got involved in many interrogations and debriefings, especially early on. I wanted to know if the evil I could imagine was sufficient for full understanding, or if I was underestimating this enemy. For many years as an intelligence officer, I always believed that if I could think it, the enemy could think it. And I came to think about some pretty evil things—maybe it was the way I grew up or maybe it came from watching movies, or maybe it was just instinctual behavior on my part. But we were facing a despicable foe, one who would rape and pillage women and children (boys and girls), and behead them for fun, all while watching pornography on their laptops. In fact, at one point, we determined that 80 percent of the material on the laptops we were capturing was pornography—these sick, psychopathic foes were unbelievably vile, but they were also guileful and cunning. If we were to beat them, we needed to outwork and outwit them.

I remember how one particular series of interrogations in 2006 showed me what we were up against—an insurgency driven not just by people, but also an idea.

██████ forces had conducted a raid on a safe house belonging to al-Qaeda in Iraq (AQI) and captured a dozen of their senior operatives. They were responsible for a highly sophisticated network managing money, logistics, transportation, propaganda, military operations, and so forth. It was impressive. And these were serious men; some of them had advanced degrees. I couldn't figure out why they were so devoted to tearing up their own country. I could understand why they wanted to fight us as occupiers, or whatever they wanted to call us, but they were slaughtering their neighbors.

Then I realized why these Sunni Arab fighters had no problem committing horrific acts against Shiites or even fellow Sunnis. They were committed to their belief system, a rigid religious and political framework based on how the founding generation of Muslim leaders, more than a century ago, ordered their world.

As I later told one interviewer, I concluded that "core al-Qaeda" wasn't actually comprised of human beings, but rather it was an ideology with a particular extremist version of Islam at its center.

More than a religion, this ideology encompasses a political belief system, because its adherents want to rule things—a village, a city, a region, or an entire caliphate—to achieve that goal, they are willing to use extreme violence. The religious nature of that threat has made it very hard for people like us who are raised in a generally secular society to come to grips with it.

They were grounded in this more or less medieval belief system, but at the same time, they'd managed to adopt modern technology to advance their goals. They were very adaptive, with networks and subnetworks interconnected to communicate internally and incorporate lessons, and failures, as well as successes.

What we found out is that very little of what they do is truly secret. They publish everything in online magazines and other media to thousands and thousands of followers. It's part of how they instruct their cadres to lead. We have always gone after the leaders, and they knew that right up front. So they placed high importance on nurturing subleaders and small groups of teams to take on the cause. That is, they were always building infrastructure, and all connected by the same message or idea, about that extremist version of Islam.

As I came to understand the enemy, I also started to see our problems as intelligence officers in more depth.

First, we addressed how we collected intelligence. I sent our soldiers out into the field. They had to understand the culture and environment in order to make the intelligence they were collecting make sense. For instance, they had to know: Who were the leaders and big men of the villages and surrounding areas? They had to know what was going on within a particular community. Let's say your intelligence was coming from one group or clan, and it was about another clan. Was that real intelligence or score-settling, or somewhere in between? They had to know these details because that information helped them understand the intelligence. And getting out in the field meant knowing the people themselves and earning their trust. Because that trust was rewarded with good intelligence.

We also saw that we needed to move much faster. Our intelligence system was not responding to the needs of 100,000-plus forces, including international forces, so we had to change how the intelligence system works.

Here's how it was in the beginning. Our team or other soldiers collected intelligence in the field that would help warfighters in the field. But it wasn't getting to them in a timely fashion. The intelligence had to go through Washington first and cycle through the bureaucracies. There are a lot of great patriots doing important work inside those agencies in Washington. I'm not saying they themselves were the problem, it was the system, so the way to fix the system was by cutting out the middleman to make sure the warfighters had the intelligence they needed when they needed it.

ALLIES IN WASHINGTON

I found plenty of allies, both inside the military and outside. I was privileged to work with some truly great people, including a few who would later play an important role in my life, like FBI agent Robyn Gritz.

We were connected in 2005 when I was in Iraq, and she was working out of FBI headquarters in Washington, in the international terrorism operations section one. That unit handled all the top terrorism cases—including al-Qaeda, fighters in Pakistan, Afghanistan, and elsewhere. We started working together a lot because she wanted to give us what we needed to fight terror. We ended up having a great and successful partnership.

She was a top-notch agent. She won all sorts of awards for her work, including one from the director of national intelligence, but she was getting beat up constantly. At some point a few years later, Robyn began to run into a headwind in her headquarters, and the name of that wind was Andrew McCabe. He wasn't deputy director yet, but he was rising in the FBI ranks fairly rapidly.

Later on, when I was director of the Defense Intelligence Agency (DIA), I wrote a letter of support for Robyn in her sexual harassment case against certain leaders in the FBI who had treated her less than professionally[8] (and may still to this day).

It was around the same time I first worked with Robyn that I first met Devin Nunes. Later on, as chairman of the House Intelligence Committee, he led the investigation into FBI abuses during its investigation of me and three other members of the Trump campaign. But when we first met, Devin was a young congressman from the Central Valley of California who was visiting Iraq on a national security delegation with Republican House Leader, and later House Speaker,

---

8   "Did the FBI Retaliate against Michael Flynn by Launching a Russia Probe?" Circa, June 27, 2017, Wayback Machine, https://web.archive.org/web/20180107122844/https://www.circa.com/story/2017/06/27/nation/did-the-fbi-retaliate-against-michael-flynn-by-launching-russia-probe.

John Boehner. Devin and I met several times during the 2006–2008 period, sometimes in Iraq, Kuwait, or back in Washington.

Devin was especially interested in the capabilities we were building to track terrorists using their personal electronic devices. It was a relatively new technology, and the terrorists didn't know we had that kind of capability. I told him that in looking for a particular individual, we were using these new tools to find the surrounding terror networks. We were eliminating terrorists and their whole network from the battlefield in large chunks at a time. For instance, using these newly developed electronic techniques, we went from doing two to three combat raids a night to twenty to thirty raids a night.

We were also able to fuse intelligence from our newly developed interrogation process with advanced communications technology and effective operations on the battlefield. In the end, we "operationalized intelligence" to increase our knowledge of the various enemies we faced and significantly sped up the exploitation and analysis components of the intelligence system, all to the benefit of our tactical to strategic decision makers.

Interrogations were enormously important, and as the new system evolved, we increased the number and quality of our interrogators. All our hard work led to a new kind of intelligence system that constantly meshed with our battlefield actions. Intelligence had to drive operations, if possible, within a single day because the terrorists were very fast. For us to dominate the battlefield, our fighting teams needed the most significant and up-to-date intelligence so they could pinpoint their next logical attack. For that to happen, we couldn't do intelligence the old way; there simply wasn't time for the information to move through the various bureaucratic levels, nor could our fighters wait for guidance. We had to do something quite different: The intelligence people had to be linked together with our operators, and they had to get the results of their fighting almost immediately.

There was still more to do. We needed to get rid of the bureaucratic bottlenecks, within our task force, more broadly within the various military services, and, perhaps most difficult, between the three-letter intelligence agencies that were working, analyzing, and fighting but doing so in their own stove-piped systems: National Security Agency (NSA), Central Intelligence Agency (CIA), Defense Intelligence Agency (DIA), and so forth. This meant undoing the traditional chain of command because, at the end of the day, our men in the field had to be able to act on the intelligence they were getting. The terrorists were fast, and we had to be faster.

Two examples that bring this need for speed to light are the use of a national jewel called the National Media Exploitation Center (NMEC) located in Washington, DC. This organization was doing some amazing work. They were taking captured material and turning it around to us as fast as they could, in days and weeks at the time—and this was fast—but it had to be faster.

Then director of NMEC, Roy Apseloff, and I figured out a way to build an electronic bridge directly between NMEC in Washington, DC, and our task force headquarters in Balad, Iraq. Once we got this bridge in place, we exponentially sped up our exploitation process and turned information around, now in minutes and hours instead of days and weeks. This adaptation broke through so many layers of bureaucracy, was done without orders and long bureaucratic processes or permission, and helped us accomplish our mission. It was accomplished only through personal relationships—sadly, the entire war had to be fought like this. Left to its own traditional devices, the bureaucracy, at all levels and, maddeningly, at every opportunity, would crush adaptation and ingenuity and result in failure. Sadly, in the end, both conflicts in Iraq and Afghanistan resulted in strategic failure.

The second example was more tactical but just as effective. In the early days, during interrogations, we would bring paper maps into the interrogation booth. The maps would be used with the detainees to get them to point out locations of certain places we were interested in finding out about. One day, we were sitting around talking about the use of Google Maps by some of our operators and tactical units because the larger imagery system wasn't working fast enough to respond to our requirements. Google Maps was a relatively new technology and software that was available on the open market.

One of our great interrogators asked, "Why can't we use this technology during interrogations?" So we taught detainees how to use a mouse with a laptop. Then we went to "Hollywood" and actually put up large flat-panel screens in the interrogation booths. Overnight, we got exponentially more fidelity of the locations we were interested in and much more accuracy for our targeting. Better still, the detainees actually liked using it. It seemed fun to them, it reinforced their fears and suspicions that the Americans knew everything and could see everything, and it made the interrogations faster. The resulting information could be electronically tracked from the interrogation booth, right out to the analytic floor, and in a digital flash right down to the operators on the battlefield.

It was an amazing application of technology and shows you that real innovation can be conjured up by smart, highly motivated American soldiers on a battlefield. We were trying to save our operators' lives, destroy our enemies, and win the damn war. To do this, our network had to be faster, more agile, and more relentless than the enemy network we were facing.

It was in using those capabilities that within a couple of years, we had eliminated a lot of al-Qaeda. The work we did in Iraq is the reason why former Congressman Devin Nunes, Generals McChrystal and Petraeus, and others gave me a large part of the credit for the "surge" in Iraq—credit I found humbling but not expected. The real credit goes to those men and women in our military who paid the ultimate sacrifice.

FIXING INTEL

The work we did in Iraq and Afghanistan streamlining the intelligence system to take enemies off the field became the basis of a study on the problems with intelligence on the battlefield. The report was titled *Fixing Intel: A Blueprint for Making Intelligence Relevant in*

Afghanistan.[9] It was published in January 2010, and I wrote it with two coauthors. My first coauthor was Marine Corps Captain Matthew Pottinger, a terrific officer and a terrific person. In his earlier life, he'd been an accomplished journalist at *The Wall Street Journal* who focused mostly on Asia. But with 9/11 he joined the Marine Corps to serve his country. He later came to work for me in the Trump administration on the National Security Council staff and did great work on China.

My other coauthor was ██████████████, a senior intelligence officer with the Defense Intelligence Agency. ████ and I worked together in the Pentagon for the chairman of the Joint Chiefs of Staff. His brother ████ is a radio talk-show host who was one of the few nationally syndicated voices who saw through the Russiagate nonsense from the very start. He gave his listeners great insight and information on the entire Russiagate operation, including my situation. Interestingly, Matt had been a frequent guest on ████████████████ show when he was a journalist.

████, Matt, and I worked on the report for months at the end of 2009. At the time, I was back in Afghanistan for my second tour there as the senior intelligence officer for that theater of operations. I thought it was important to do my own assessment and see the battlefield as a whole. And given the nature of that war, it meant looking at the entire country. I went to almost every town and village to do my own assessment.

I came to know Afghanistan very well—walking it, driving it, and scouting it from above as we helicoptered into places to meet with Afghans. I even met with a number of Taliban officials, as well as the former ambassador for al-Qaida to Pakistan. Since I was the senior intelligence officer, they wanted to meet with me, and I wanted to

9   Matt Pottinger, Michael T. Flynn, ██████████████, "Fixing Intel: A Blueprint for Making Intelligence Relevant in Afghanistan," Center for a New American Security, January 4, 2020, https://www.cnas.org/publications/reports/fixing-intel-a-blueprint-for-making-intelligence-relevant.

meet with them to determine what was going on. Many people didn't like that back in Washington, DC, but I'm on the battlefield trying to learn and see as much as I can to help our soldiers know the terrain and win.

In mid-July 2009, I took a small team back around the country examining the intelligence operations in a far more detailed way. Speaking to many of the Afghan people as far down into the various villages as we could was essential. I also started to develop relationships during this period with some very notorious characters, like then-Colonel Raziq of Spin Boldak in southern Kandahar Province.

Raziq was known for his narcotics and poppy smuggling down across the Pakistan border at a place called "Friendship Gate." This place was anything but friendly. He was a slim, very wiry, and extremely tough guy. He showed me a couple of bullet wounds he had taken fighting the Taliban. Most Americans likely only see such a person in a National Geographic magazine. The Taliban had killed at least two of his brothers and had tried to kill him on more than one occasion. Despite his many unsavory characteristics, I liked Raziq; he was very straightforward with me, as I was with him.

I didn't like what he represented nor what he did, but we needed him badly. He maintained stability in his tribal areas. He knew what was needed, and he ruled with an iron fist. He also knew things our troops desperately had to know. I traveled with him in a beat-up Toyota truck one day through his turf. As we drove through some villages, he would veer off-road and along what can only be described as a path that, he knew, was clear of mines and other explosives. Men and young children (girls and boys) would come up to him, and he would hand out Afghan money to them. I felt like I was with someone out of a Robin Hood story. They loved him.

He showed me that the human terrain in Afghanistan, and the fabric of the society, was vastly different from Iraq, and we could not impose similar actions on this ecosystem like we had in Iraq. Getting tribal leaders to come over to our side was going to be very difficult, and if we were going to use this type of approach, we would have to work this hard in multiple areas of the country and with multiple tribal leaders.

What we learned in Afghanistan and Iraq was documented in *Fixing Intel*. And we argued that our lessons should be incorporated across our entire military and intelligence to make things more efficient and more effective.

The report was also seen as an indictment of the intelligence community, which was true—it was. But I was criticizing something I was part of. If I wasn't worried about criticizing myself, why would I worry about bruising other egos? We'd been at war for nearly a decade and were doing it backward. My hope was that it wasn't too late to get it right.

Still, *Fixing Intel* created an uproar, especially back in Washington. There were demands to fire me, and there was lots of hate mail coming in too. It was nothing compared to what I later went through with the lies about Russiagate, but it was bad enough. Eventually, it was the Obama administration's Secretary of Defense Robert Gates who calmed everyone down. He said the report was brilliant and that we should take a look at what Flynn is recommending.

Gates consulted with the director of national intelligence, a man who later played a major role in my public persecution, Air Force General James Clapper. It was Clapper who told me shortly after *Fixing Intel* was published that he was calling me back to Washington to fix all the problems I'd described in the report.[10] Some of them we did solve, and it saved American lives. But there was a different problem-set I was about to run into for the first time back in the capital of the free world.

---

10 "Defense Intelligence Agency Leadership Change Ceremony," C-SPAN, July 23, 2012, timestamp 41:03-41:18, https://www.c-span.org/program/public-affairs-event/defense-intelligence-agency-leadership-change-ceremony/282717.

CHAPTER 5

DIRECTING INTELLIGENCE

COMING TO WASHINGTON

In the fall of 2011, I returned stateside to take a new job in Washington, DC, as assistant director of National Intelligence (DNI) for partner engagement. I was working for James Clapper. This assignment entailed strengthening existing and building new intelligence relationships with foreign allies and partners across the international community, and all our federal, state, and American Indian tribal partners across the United States. I worked on a daily basis with Jim Clapper. He and I had a good relationship—I thought one where he could trust me, and I trusted him. That turned out to be a huge error in my judgment later on after my departure from government and getting politically involved in the Trump campaign and presidency. Jim Clapper turned out to be among those useful idiots who was used by the Obama administration for the purposes of promoting a massive lie.[11] Jim carried the water instead of demonstrating courage to tell the truth.

During this time, I was promoted to lieutenant general, which requires an appointment from the president of the United States. It was the first of my two presidential appointments under President Obama. The second was in April 2012, when I was nominated to become director of the Defense Intelligence Agency (DIA).

Both appointments entailed a lengthy process including investigations, background checks, and finally Senate confirmation. I was vet-

---

11 Doug G. Ware, "Sally Yates, James Clapper: Trump White House Warned about Flynn," UPI, May 8, 2017, https://www.upi.com/Top_News/US/2017/05/08/Sally-Yates-James-Clapper-Trump-White-House-warned-about-Flynn/1941494268722/.

ted inside out. The idea that I'd been hiding some secret relationship with a foreign power—as the media, political operatives, and former colleagues in the intelligence community would later claim—is nuts.

I started at DIA in July and hit the ground running. I'd reached the highest levels of the US intelligence community and was hopeful that I could effect some changes, in line with what I'd described in *Fixing Intel*. One of the most important changes I put into place at DIA was instituting the idea of "intelligence centers" focused on supporting our four-star warfighting commands. On the battlefield, we created interagency task forces and merged them into effective intelligence fusion centers, and I was determined to do the same in my role as head of all defense intelligence. To this day, the center concept that our leadership team and I implemented remains in place. That alone is a seminal accomplishment in bureaucracies. This initiative was so crucial for integrating various intelligence components across the broader intelligence community that some years later, CIA Director John Brennan did the same at his agency.

For me, years later, the media offered nothing but grief for my push to integrate intelligence across the government in support of our most precious resources, the men and women still engaged in combat operations around the world, especially in Iraq and Afghanistan. For Brennan, he was touted in the controlled media as being an innovator. I didn't care about the credit; what I cared about was creating an environment to produce more effective intelligence, and we did.

When I arrived at DIA, the culture was still not focused on warfighting. Too many at the DIA headquarters were still focused on pretending to be the CIA instead of focused on warfighting—our principle and DOD-directed mission. I wanted to change the culture to have more of a downward focus on the warfighting commands, with priorities going to our deployed forces in the Middle East and Central Asia. This was a giant hurdle and came with internal squabbling by senior bureaucrats in the agency and from others across the Washington, DC, community.

People in Washington get comfortable in their cubicles and don't want their lives disrupted for minor things like wars or significant combat operations. Many are more worried about their next promotion or their job title or which social event they'll get invited to. People in Washington are enamored by office titles—the longer and more complex, the more prestige they feel about themselves.

The culture at DIA needed to be refocused on warfighting. That is what Secretary of Defense Leon Panetta told me during my initial office call prior to taking over DIA, and that is what Jim Clapper told me to fix as well. DIA culture was too driven by what Washington insiders described instead of what our warfighting commanders needed. That changed over the time I was there, and all the commanders I spoke to routinely told me they appreciated the direct support they felt coming from their DIA people and other assets.

In fact, early on Clapper and I talked about solving some of the intelligence community's bureaucratic problems that I'd described in *Fixing Intel*. I had a decent relationship with Clapper; we spoke regularly and met when I wasn't traveling overseas or around the country. I interacted with the CIA, too, and met with the agency's director, John Brennan. I did not care for Brennan. He's a pompous ass and self-serving. He did me no favors while I was at DIA. In fact, he made my time there more difficult by blocking what I wanted to do. Sadly, Jim Clapper allowed Brennan to run circles around him, and he did.

I also interacted regularly with the FBI director at the time, Robert Mueller. I thought Mueller was a decent man, but I always felt he was out of touch. His deputy, Sean Joyce, an aggressive but sharp senior agent, pretty much ran the organization. Then Mueller retired and was replaced by James Comey, who is cut from the same cloth as Brennan. They called him the "Cardinal" at the FBI because of his sanctimonious and pompous attitude toward regular Americans and his abuse of the rule of law: leveraging the FBI as his own personal tool to attack designated enemies of Obama.

Of course, I had no idea how large a role—or how negative a role—any of these people would come to play in my life within only two short years.

It was during this period that I started to understand the sprawling nature of the national intelligence community. I'd written about the problems with the Washington-based agencies in *Fixing Intel*, but until I was working alongside them, running one of the largest intelligence agencies in the world, I had little sense these institutions had become sort of like a government in itself.

I locked horns with the CIA about sharing classified information with the people who needed it most—our warfighters out in the field. I had some of these same issues when I deployed on the battlefield as well. Their obsession with protecting sources and methods was smoke and mirrors for their many failings as a covert intelligence collection agency. Often they didn't have good sources, and their methods were pathetic. They weren't that good. I knew what intelligence the CIA had because at that level I had the clearances to get access to it. As I was reading some of it, I was thinking, *We should be sharing it with the guys downrange, our combat soldiers.* When I asked whether our units in Afghanistan and Iraq had this information, the people briefing me didn't know.

I'd tell them, "Well, you better go find out. Find out right now. Call up so-and-so." I would pick up the phone and call up the commander, or I'd call up the people on the ground whom I knew, usually, the senior intelligence officers, and I would say, "Hey, you need to pull reports X, Y, Z." I would give them a summary over a secure phone call. I would tell them what I had just read, and I would say this is dangerous. They needed to be aware of it, because I had that sense of urgency. That sense of urgency comes from my many years deployed supporting combat operations. Back in cushy Washington, there is no sense of urgency. There is only another three-day weekend to look forward to. On the battlefield, there are no three-day weekends.

The warfighters needed to know what al-Qaeda knew about our operations. How did al-Qaeda run counterintelligence operations, for example? What were their spying and other intelligence collection efforts inside of our formations? Among the major issues I took on at DIA was increasing our human intelligence footprint across the globe. Human intelligence is something the DIA is experienced with, but the CIA sees these operations as their sole purview. They are overly and unnecessarily protective to the point of being useless and careless, especially when it comes to foreign counterintelligence efforts directed against US forces. DIA needed its defense capabilities to support its roles and missions. But to the nation's detriment, the CIA sees itself as the "pros from Dover," and they are anything but.

OFFICIAL TRIP TO MOSCOW

The DIA is responsible for all defense attachés working out of over 140 U.S. embassies around the world. The director of DIA is also the head of the Defense Foreign Attachés Corps in Washington, DC, as well as responsible for all US defense attachés globally.

Among the key attaché offices are London, Beijing, Cairo, and Moscow, and because of the importance of those embassies, we have general officers assigned to them. My defense attaché in the Moscow embassy was Brigadier General Pete Zwack.

I conducted an approved USG visit in June 2013, and Pete set up a series of important meetings for me with my Russian counterpart, Lieutenant General Igor Sergun, head of Russian military intelligence, the GRU, which is roughly the equivalent of the DIA. My visit had been fully briefed and approved all the way up to the DNI, and I was told the White House was also aware of the trip.

US-Russia relationships at the time were not great, and my trip was an important one to help rebuild relationships with at least the Russian military. Once we arrived, we had meetings at our US embassy to get briefed on the various players and to gain some of the on-the-ground experiences and personal descriptions of who some of the key players were.

We went to the GRU's headquarters, an ultramodern building, for a series of meetings that started with a face-to-face with General Sergun to get to know each other.

He and I immediately hit it off. We were both combat veterans who'd fought against radical Islamists in different parts of the world. His time was spent mainly in Chechnya, mine in Afghanistan and Iraq. We were both roughly the same age. We each had two children; he had two daughters, and I had two sons. We joked about bureaucrats and politicians and about how similar our lives had been growing up as soldiers. He was a very reasonable guy, a good guy. He was clearly smart and someone I felt very comfortable with. There were things our two sides disagreed on, but we shared concerns on major issues, especially radical Islamic terrorism. And I was hopeful we could work together on some of these problems.

This was the first time that someone at my level, or anyone for that matter, had visited GRU headquarters, and we were grateful. We discussed how important this was for him to have received permission for me to be invited inside this important organization's inner sanctuary. He and I developed an initial rapport during that first meeting, and the rest of the visit went very well.

Our delegation visited with his primary staff and briefly with his boss, the chairman of their joint chiefs. We visited their war memorial museum and the tomb of the unknown soldier at Moscow's version of Arlington Cemetery, where I participated in a wreath-laying ceremony.

It was a long day in face-to-face meetings in his office and conference room, where I gave an hour-long presentation to his entire staff, approximately fifty officers. I spoke on a variety of topics, such as lessons learned from our experiences in the war, but principally on leadership and intelligence in war. These Russian military intelligence officers had never met a US military intelligence official at my level.

That night we hosted a dinner at Pete's residence at the US embassy, and Sergun brought two generals and an interpreter. We toasted to our continued efforts to find issues to work together on—we toasted to making "the airlocks fit," which referred to the Apollo-Soyuz linkup during the heart of the Cold War in 1975. Sergun liked that. Both sides wanted to improve relations. The Russians left with US embassy baseball caps for their kids. The next night, our last in Moscow, Sergun hosted us at the Sovietsky Hotel, where he gave us a tour of an upstairs suite where Stalin had stayed.

Overall the visit was a major success. It was a big deal because it showed how much we and the Russians had in common. And that was the point of the trip: We wanted to develop a relationship with the Russians through whatever means we could. Being DIA director opened the door, and Sergun and I were on our way to building a relationship because we respected each other's military career, in particular our combat experiences fighting terrorists.

I invited Sergun and his staff to visit Washington, DC, and they scheduled a trip for February 2014. But it was canceled after the Russians invaded Crimea. I argued that it was because of the war in Ukraine that it would still be a good thing to continue this dialogue. I knew our diplomatic and political relationships with Russia weren't very strong, and I felt this relationship offered a strategic touchpoint to keep dialogue open. But my bosses Jim Clapper and Mike Vickers, the undersecretary of defense for intelligence, said no. I felt that was a mistake. Keeping dialogue open at such a critical time was essential, and always is, but the Obama administration had different ideas.

Sadly, General Sergun died of a heart attack in January 2016 while visiting Russian forces who were based in Syria supporting the Bashar al-Assad regime. The Russian general was a good, tough soldier and leader. We only spent a very brief time together, but we connected. Over time, I think that our relationship might have grown stronger and, with it, maybe the ties between our two countries.

But it's obvious that today our relationship with Russia has deteriorated almost entirely—which is why I've gone into such detail about this US government–approved trip. In my judgment, the Obama administration missed a major opportunity.

Obviously, Russiagate was destructive for me and my family, and for the Trump presidency as a whole. For two years, the Mueller investigation basically neutralized the man Americans elected to implement the policies he promised to enact on the campaign trail. That's everything from building the wall to stemming the tide of illegal immigrants to decoupling us from China and returning jobs to our shores. But Russiagate also represents an enormous foreign policy disaster.

Obama, Clinton, their Deep State corps, and the media made it nearly impossible for the Trump administration to have ordinary relations with Russia. Instead, the political operation weaponized to destroy their political opponent at home has put us in a very dangerous situation with a foreign power that has an enormous nuclear arsenal. The lines of communication that I was hoping to build are now nonexistent.

Because the Democrats believed—or have to pretend to believe—their own lie that Vladimir Putin helped put Trump in the White House, they see the Russian leader as a uniquely evil figure in world history who has to be destroyed. In their view, there can be no accommodation with Russia, not even a line of communication. I'm not saying Putin is a good guy—that is not mine to judge. But we need to be able to speak to Russia and its leaders. Instead, we have a disastrous, and potentially apocalyptic, framework for US policy toward Moscow, especially now with the Biden administration supporting Ukraine in its proxy war against Russia.

DINNER IN CAMBRIDGE

The Russiagate narrative drew on another trip I made as DIA director—this one to Cambridge, England, home of one of the world's most famous educational institutions, Cambridge University. DIA at the time had a small number of students attending Cambridge as doctoral candidates, degrees the agency pays for. It's a very prestigious, hand-selected group, and the primary reason I visited Cambridge February 28, 2014, was to see them.

It was a very long day of presentations and discussions, mostly with students and some faculty, as well as some residents from the local area. There were a few hundred people in attendance. In the evening, there was a formal reception and sit-down dinner with a small group of students, some of whom were part of DIA, and others were faculty and staff from Cambridge.

Our host for the evening was Sir Richard Dearlove, the former head of the United Kingdom's foreign intelligence service, MI6. In the lead-up to the Iraq war, he, too, had given his political superiors unverified intelligence about Saddam Hussein's WMD. After retiring from MI6 in 2004, Dearlove became the master of one of Cambridge's residential colleges, Pembroke.

He came across more as a professor than the former "spymaster" of Great Britain. He was a likable man, grandfatherly. He was well-read and had a good grasp of the global situation, especially the wars in the Middle East. He had a negative attitude toward NATO and understood the role the UK should play in world affairs. I felt that we connected.

The dinner was late because the day had already been very long like most days on the road were for me. After dinner, my DIA liaison, ███████████, and I departed and returned to our hotel. In all, it was a totally unremarkable but pleasant visit at Cambridge. But that's not how the media described it three years later when reports claimed that I'd had a suspicious meeting with a Russian national.

One of the Cambridge students who attended the events of the day as well as the dinner was a British and Russian national named Svetlana Lokhova. I remember that we spoke briefly. I also remember she was pregnant and getting ready to start a family. She later became acquaintances with members of my family, especially my brothers Joe and Jack, after what she went through. She wasn't a spy. She was a graduate student and a young mother, but they dragged her name through the mud, ruined her career, and forever changed her life.

I'll go into what my family went through regarding this episode in fuller detail in a later chapter. For now, it's enough to say that three years after the dinner, US and UK government agents used her attendance at the dinner to insinuate I had some connection to her and claim I'd been compromised by Russian intelligence.

This ridiculous narrative seems to have started with Stefan Halper,[12] a long-time US intelligence asset and political insider who taught at Cambridge. His former father-in-law, Ray Cline, had been a significant figure in the CIA's early days, and Halper let on to Cambridge students that he himself was a hot-shot intelligence operative. But in reality, he was just an FBI informant.[13] And it seems his real specialty was running dirty tricks operations for political campaigns. What the press never reported was that Halper wasn't even at the dinner that Dearlove hosted. Of course that didn't matter to the media hordes that jumped all over Halper's account when the Russiagate narrative poisoned the brains of millions of Americans.

The purpose of Halper's fake story was to suggest I'd been caught in a Russian honey trap. Spies look for a target's weakness. Maybe it's women or alcohol or gambling, and they set you up. Next thing you know, you wake up, and you're compromised. That really does happen.

I've overseen operations that compromised people. It's part of what intelligence agencies call tradecraft. I know specific examples in combat where we would do that because we wanted somebody to give us information about the enemies and the leadership we were going after. This happens at all levels. If we put somebody into a compromising position overseas, we show them things we know about them and say, "Well, look, now you're going to work for me."

---

12 "Judge says Halper Made Misstatements to the FBI About General Flynn," Epoch Times, 2023, https://www.youtube.com/watch?v=9MnMmgE80Ys&t=38s

13 *United States of America v. Michael T. Flynn*, United States District Court, District of Columbia, Case 1:17-cr-00232-EGS, Document 189, filed April 30, 2020, pg. 17, https://static1.squarespace.com/static/5e80e0d236405d1c7b8eaec9/t/5eab8abb0d051f73 1cfe87e2/1588300482261/Doc.+189+Flynn+SECOND+SUPPLEMENT+TO+MOTION+ TO+DISMISS+FOR+EGREGIOUS+GOVERNMENT+MISCONDUCTpdf.

Maybe we offer to pay them in exchange for information about a lab they work in or the weapon system they're helping develop.

We try to compromise them, and they try to compromise us. Our adversaries are very serious about hurting America, and they don't have any rules. They don't worry about drugging somebody or somebody sticking a couple of young boys in a room with a US senator or congressman, for instance. Nearly every politician in Washington, DC, has vulnerabilities and weaknesses, and sometimes they're caught in that moment of vulnerability, and then they're compromised. It happens all the time in Washington, DC, and it's not just our enemies, like Russia and China, who are doing it. Sometimes it's our own government compromising our own people.

And sometimes our government turns on its own citizens, its own public servants, its own combat veterans, just because it's acting out of vengeance. That's what happened in my case. I didn't have any weaknesses or vulnerabilities like women or booze or anything like that. They tried to invent one with the story they later told about the 2014 Cambridge dinner.

They came after me because I told the truth. I said that America and Americans were in danger, and I was punished for it. It wasn't enough that I was asked to resign from my post after I told the truth and challenged Obama's political narrative. No, they opened the gates of hell on me and my family.

TELLING AMERICANS THE TRUTH

It may seem strange to people who associate me now with the America First movement, but I was a registered Democrat. We were a lower-middle-class Irish Catholic family from New England, and we saw Republicans as the country club party, the party of the people who looked down on us. I was born three years before John F. Kennedy was elected president, but I grew up around family, friends, and neighbors who thought an Irish Catholic president of the United States was a dream come true. So we were Kennedy Democrats. I was a Kennedy Democrat.

My point is that when it was time to fulfill my duty as DIA director to give Congress the agency's assessment of the threats to America, the last thing on my mind was to make a political statement. I'm a soldier. When I testified before the United States Senate and House of Representatives, I wasn't trying to undermine the political narrative of a Democratic administration. I just told the truth.

The approved narrative was that al-Qaeda was on the run. But that wasn't true. When Obama and his deputies said that "al-Qaeda's on the run,"[14] they were doing a disservice to the American public. They kept going back to killing bin Laden. But what did killing him really do? It would have been better to capture the guy, interrogate him, and expose how he uses Islamic ideology for his own purposes.

Killing him just gave our enemies a martyr to exploit for propaganda purposes.

The truth was, things weren't going so hot in 2014. Al-Qaeda seemed like less of a problem in part because of the way the organization had rebranded its subsidiaries. Al-Qaeda told their different affiliates not to use the name "al-Qaeda" since that would only draw more attention to them, especially from us. Boko Haram, for example, is a rebranding of the Nigerian branch of al-Qaeda that was told not to use the name.

But just because the name al-Qaeda was less in circulation didn't mean that Sunni jihadis had left the stage. Just the opposite. In fact, the enemy was growing. They were expanding.

Every time we dropped a bomb on a terrorist's head, we created ten more. That's what was happening because of our drone campaign. We were sending drones to kill people around the Middle East, North Africa, and Central Asia: Somalia, Afghanistan, Pakistan, Iraq, Yemen, and elsewhere. We'd kill their leadership, and they'd replace him with someone better.

---

14 David Gregory, "May 5: Patrick Leahy, Rudy Giuliani, Jane Harman, Tom Cotton, Newt Gingrich, Harold Ford Jr., Rich Lowry, Joy-Ann Reid, Brendon Ayanbadejo," NBC News, May 5, 2013, https://www.nbcnews.com/id/wbna51778950.

There was something even worse that my agency was tracking—the growth of a new and very dangerous organization that had first begun to appear in Iraq and Syria known as the Islamic State (ISIS). At first, it comprised former al-Qaeda fighters, like its so-called caliph, Abu-Bakr al-Baghdadi, as well as former military officials from Saddam Hussein's regime, like Izzat Ibrahim al-Douri, a former high-level Baath party official. Then ISIS began to expand rapidly. At the time, they had branches in twenty-four nations, from West Africa to Indonesia and the Philippines. And their operations were becoming more and more horrific.

In short, we weren't winning. In 2014, every commander who came out of Afghanistan or Iraq said, "We've accomplished our mission." They said the same thing every year, but that didn't mean we were winning. We weren't. The administration shaped the narrative to show we were winning, but I knew we weren't. So in the early winter of 2014 when I was scheduled to give three briefs in three successive weeks on Capitol Hill assessing worldwide threats that could affect America and US national security, I told the truth.

As part of the procedure, my statement went to the DNI and the White House for vetting. It was returned to me the night before the first hearing, January 29.

It was struck through with red lines to change my testimony. That also amounted to changing the assessment coming from DIA. With nearly thirty-three years of experience behind me, I'm thinking, What the hell is going on? I turned to my DIA congressional affairs officer, ████████, and asked what he thought. He told me that he had never seen anything like this before either. I told him to print a clean copy of the original report and get it back to me.

On the day of the hearing, Comey, Brennan, and Clapper all showed up with their large teams of staffers. I remembered I was at that famous Senate hearing with Clapper back in March 2013 when Senator Ron Wyden (D-OR) asked if the intelligence community was spying on Americans. Clapper squirmed in his chair. "No, sir," he said. "Not wittingly."

What did that mean? Did it mean that we were spying on Americans by mistake, and even after they found out, they kept doing it...by mistake? No, what it meant was: Yes, we are spying on Americans, and we're not going to admit it. Not publicly, for sure. And even in a classified setting, we'll throw chaff at you because we are responsible to no one but ourselves—certainly not to the American people and their representatives. "Not wittingly." The phrase represents everything that was wrong with the agencies.

But my job was to find out what our adversaries were up to in order to protect the American people and tell the American public the truth about what we were doing by informing their elected representatives.

The three other directors were asked a series of questions and kept to the approved narrative—al-Qaeda was on the run. When I was asked the same questions, I told them how our agency assessed worldwide threats in 2014, an assessment that showed Sunni jihadism was growing and that we weren't winning. When I was asked if al-Qaeda was on the run, like the administration was messaging, I responded simply, "No."

The photographs from the testimony capture some of the emotions of the other directors—Clapper, Brennan, and Comey were surprised, maybe shocked, I wasn't sticking with the preapproved narrative. But the narrative is designed to serve political interests, and when you're at war if your priority is to control the message, you're putting lives at risk, in particular the lives of those you've sent into a warzone. So, I told the truth.

Shortly after I gave my testimony, I was called into a meeting at the Pentagon with Jim Clapper and Mike Vickers, the undersecretary of defense for intelligence. Vickers has an interesting reputation from his own service in uniform up until he joined the civilian bureaucracy. He was my immediate civilian boss on the defense side, but to no one's surprise, the DIA director has many bosses.

Vickers is a smart guy but with a very strange sort of personality—he always struck me as the type of guy that has a secret he's keeping from you. I worked with and for many great leaders in my time, but he was not among them. I later learned how he was undermining me at DIA by manipulating some of my subordinate senior executives, one of whom was my immediate deputy, and CIA officer, David Shedd.

During the meeting with Vickers and Clapper, the latter said, "We're going to ask you to step down." Normally the DIA director's job is a three-year appointment. At the time, I was almost two years into it. I immediately asked, "Is it because of my leadership?"

I wanted to make sure it had nothing to do with my job as a leader. Later there was a lot of noise in the media about how I did a poor job leading the agency, but that wasn't true at all.

"Oh, no, it's not your leadership," said Clapper. "If it was, I'd cut you off at the knees right now, and you wouldn't go back into the job." He said it was because of my attitude. In other words, they were removing me because I wasn't playing ball. I hadn't supported the political message that the political officials wanted to send to cover their failures.

Once I realized why they were asking me to leave DIA early, I realized I needed to slow this meeting down. As a three-star general, you need to have served at that rank for a certain period of time to keep that rank when you retire. This was important: I had earned my three stars, and I was being pushed out for political reasons. If forced to retire immediately, I would have had to retire as a two-star general. These two didn't care, and I knew that no one in the Obama administration was going to step up to help me.

So, I asked Clapper if I could finish two complete years, which would take me to August 2014. He agreed, and Vickers nodded like a bobblehead doll.

Never in my career had I worked for "leaders" who failed to stand up for their subordinates, something I had done many times over in the many leadership positions I held. Here I was with two of the top officials in the US intelligence community. I stood there based on truth and principles, and they were sitting there focused on being politically correct. Political correctness is a major problem across the entire US government, and most certainly across the US intelligence community, and it's just become worse. This now weaponized "political correctness" is systematically destroying the fabric of our country.

I wondered how Jim Clapper had changed. He was the one who brought me in and pushed for me to be in those critical positions. And now I was out, not because I'd failed at my job but because I hadn't served the administration's political narrative.

After Clapper agreed that I'd stay until August, I walked out of the room and called Lori. "Honey," I said, "things are going to change again." She was probably a little relieved. Finally, no more moving around. It was time to retire and make my way into the private sector. I was optimistic about it. It was time to try something else and open a new chapter in my life. I'd served my country for more than thirty-three years, five of those years in combat. I'd protected America and saved the lives of Americans serving abroad, from Grenada to Afghanistan. I'd shown I was one of the top intelligence officers, some say the best, of my generation. Those are pretty high and humbling marks. I reached the top of my profession, ending my career as director of the Defense Intelligence Agency and the senior military intelligence officer in the Department of Defense.

Whatever was in my future would still in some way involve speaking the truth about the dangers facing our great country. But as far as I was concerned, I was gone from government for good.

CHAPTER 6

CIVILIAN LIFE

FLYNN & SON

In April 2014 I announced my retirement effective later in the year, and in September, after thirty-three years in uniform, I left government service. There were all kinds of people approaching me with opportunities.

Typically, a general leaves the military with lots of offers to take a seat on a board of a big defense or, in my case, intelligence-related company. That's how you're thanked in Washington, DC, for serving your country. Some cog in the military-industrial and security state complex pays you millions to sit on a board and use your government contacts to advance their business interests.

I'll admit that I fell into the trap a little bit. I started to get offers from firms surrounding these complexes. Some I took, others I declined, but I always felt uneasy about retired generals using their influence to get access. For a time, I did get involved in one of the big Washington, DC, speakers' bureaus. I always enjoyed speaking to audiences, and this was something I wanted to do. I like sharing my ideas and lessons with audiences willing to listen. These speaking bureaus arrange speaking engagements and pay good money for them. I did, and still do, like to speak about issues and ideas that I knew about and were important to me, like military or intelligence issues, or foreign policy and national security issues. For the first few months after leaving government, I gave a speech once or twice a month.

But I'd spent most of my life, and all of my professional career, in the military, and I was not comfortable in the world of professional

Washington power brokers. So I set up a consulting business with my son Michael.

I wanted to spend time with him. I'd missed a lot of his life and my son Matthew's life. At the time I left the government, Matthew was deployed abroad, just like I had been for the last ten to fifteen years of my career. With the country at war, I had worked all day and night, seven days a week. I missed birthdays, anniversaries, weddings, Thanksgivings, Christmases, and Easters.

But for all that, I was lucky in one respect. In some of my postings as a junior officer, I was able to get involved with coaching my boys' youth teams, like soccer and basketball, but as you become more senior, your life isn't really your own. You have a responsibility to your mission, and your mission is your people because their lives depend on it. It doesn't mean you give up your family, but you need a strong family to understand that mission because they're actually a big part of that mission.

I was deployed overseas when my son Matthew got married, and I missed his wedding. When Michael was to be married, I flew in from Afghanistan the night before and barely made it. So when I left the military, I wanted to spend time with Michael. He was working with my brother Joe at the time, so I went to Michael and said, "Hey, let's work together. We'll figure it out as we go."

We started the Flynn Intel Group, and Michael worked his tail off to help me manage things: scheduling, overseeing transportation, setting up billing, and running a small company. In the military, especially as a senior officer, you have a staff to help you out, but when you get out of the military, you're on your own. My son was my staff and my business partner, and it was an honor to work closely with him every day. He is incredibly talented, has an extraordinary number of skills, and has a terrific personality. He's just a good person, and we had a lot of fun. He says 2015 and 2016 were some of the best years of his life getting to work with me, and I feel the same.

One of the reasons I went to Moscow for what became the infamous dinner celebrating the tenth anniversary of RT (formerly Russia

Today) was to show him some of the historic sights there that I'd seen during my previous trip to Russia in June 2013 to meet with Russian military intelligence officials.

The picture of me sitting at the dinner table with Vladimir Putin was used to make me and Putin look like best friends or collaborators. When I put aside the fact that they used it to target me and President Trump, I can say objectively that it's one of the stupidest ideas I've ever heard. You don't need to be an intelligence officer to see how dumb it is: I'm supposed to have had some covert relationship with the Russians, and the proof is that I'm sitting next to Putin at a public event with hundreds of dignitaries from around the world that was photographed by Russian and international media? Yet as ridiculous as the allegations were about the dinner, the media ate it up.

HERE'S THE REAL STORY

The event itself was the tenth anniversary of RT. My Washington, DC, speakers' bureau set up the event for me. I didn't accept all the opportunities they arranged, but I took this one. I saw this as a great way for Michael and me to travel overseas together. We'd never done that before. The event was scheduled for December 2015, just prior to the Christmas holidays, so we figured we would spend time shopping for Christmas gifts as well. And we did, also visiting an outdoor Christmas fair held in Red Square. It was an historic and terrific time for me and my son. Here I thought it would be an experience we would fondly remember for years to come. Was I wrong?

The trip involved an interview with RT correspondent Sophie Shevardnadze. We spoke in front of the forum, probably 200 people in the audience. We talked about radical Islam and the situation unfolding in the Middle East. The fake news media never mentioned these remarks because they didn't fit their narrative.

Just a few weeks before there had been a major coordinated terror attack in France targeting a soccer game, cafes in Paris, and a Paris concert hall, the Bataclan, where 90 people had been massacred. A total of 130 had been killed. The audience was very interested to hear this discussed since the Russians had also suffered tremendously from terror attacks at home, like the 2002 crisis at a Moscow theater, when 132 people had been killed.

I also discussed the negative role that Iran was playing in the Middle East and said that the Russians should play a positive role and get Iran to back out of the proxy wars they're involved in, referring specifically to Syria.

The night of the event it was freezing cold. Michael and I walked from the hotel for a reception to be followed by a formal sit-down dinner. Most everyone at my table either spoke no English or spoke it haltingly. Also it was a very loud event. Whenever there was a break between speakers, there was entertainment. I should add that it was superb. The Russian Military Chorus was exceptional. They sang for about thirty minutes, and some of their songs were clearly patriotic numbers because many in the room knew the words and sang along.

My famous meeting with Putin lasted less than ten seconds. He was announced, entered the room, and everyone stood. He walked down the center aisle to our table. He shook hands with some of us at the table, including me. Our very brief encounter was a simple and cordial greeting. He only sat for a short time, then got up and gave a speech about RT in which he thanked them for their work promoting Russia and the Russian people around the world.

Once his speech was over, he immediately departed, and the guests soon followed, including the former secretary general of the Soviet Union, Mikhail Gorbachev, and former Michigan governor, and professional wrestler, Jesse Ventura. The evening had come to an end.

My entire trip both going and upon return was briefed[15] to elements of the DIA and other US agencies. I followed all defense and intelligence community protocols and procedures for engaging in

---

15 John Solomon, "Exculpatory Russia Evidence about Mike Flynn That US Intel Kept Secret," *The Hill*, January 2, 2019, https://thehill.com/opinion/white-house/423558-exculpatory-russia-evidence-about-mike-flynn-that-us-intel-kept-secret/.

overseas events like this one. The FBI had, and still has, full access to all of this as do all other elements of the defense and intelligence communities. Clapper knew the truth; they all did. When a former director makes a trip like that, it's a huge deal. It's not just some analyst going abroad—it's the former director of the Defense Intelligence Agency going for a three-day trip to Russia. I got fully briefed prior. I debriefed after, and I provided them with things I saw, people I met, phone numbers on napkins, providing them photos and information. This is all known, yet they lied through their teeth accusing me of being a Russian spy. And to this day, I am still in a legal battle with the DOD for docking my retirement pay for the full amount I was paid for the speech. All because of their vindictiveness owing to Hillary Clinton's losing her run for the presidency.[16]

And still what sticks in my mind most about that trip isn't the insanity that followed it after I'd joined the Trump campaign but the fond memory of getting to travel with my son at Christmas time.

SPEAKING MY MIND

I made it a high priority to do as many media appearances as possible to explain to audiences around the world what the Obama administration was really up to. It was Michael who arranged most of my media appearances.

We didn't care what media outlets or what the venues were. I just asked Michael who the audience was. If it was the right audience, I wanted to do it. I wanted to make sure that my message was getting out there, and the main message was that the Obama administration wasn't telling the truth about the wars in Iraq and Afghanistan, or almost any other part of their foreign policy. I couldn't sit back and watch these people lie to the American public anymore.

---

16 Bryan Metzger, "Ex-Trump National Security Advisor Michael Flynn Was Fined $38,557 by the Army for Attending a 2015 Moscow Gala with Putin," Business Insider, July 8, 2022, https://www.businessinsider.com/michael-flynn-trump-national-security-advisor-fined-army-vladimir-putin-2022-7?utm_medium=referral&utm_source=yahoo.com.

For instance, I went on Al Jazeera and Sky News Arabia as well as many American mainstream media outlets. I criticized the Obama administration for not supporting the Syrian opposition and letting al-Qaeda branches like ISIS and al-Nusra Front and other extremists take control of the war against Assad. Another big message was to counter what the Obama administration was saying about the Iranian nuclear deal.

Shortly before the White House came to an agreement legalizing Iran's nuclear weapons program in July 2015, I went on Fox. I explained that Obama's Iran policy was one of "willful ignorance." Iran was sparking a "regional sectarian war," and Obama was adding fuel to the fire. The issue wasn't just Iranian nukes, I said. Iran is also a country with ballistic missiles and extensive cyber capabilities. They are also still a state sponsor of terrorism, and here we are dealing with them as though we're going to give them carte blanche.

I also testified on Capitol Hill about Obama's Iran deal. I wanted to show that many of the promises the White House had made to the American people about this agreement were false.

There was no way that the International Atomic Energy Administration (IAEA) would be able to verify if Iran was in compliance. IAEA inspectors didn't have full access to Iran's nuclear facilities to know whether they were unlawfully developing weapons. We wouldn't be able to "snap back" sanctions on Iran like the White House claimed. Further, the Iranians were more out of control than ever, with their rogue actions destabilizing Iraq, Syria, Lebanon, Yemen, and elsewhere.

Most important to me, I pointed out what should have been foremost on the minds of policymakers but wasn't: Iran was in the business of killing or maiming Americans during the Iraq war from the beginning in 2003 and since 2005 aided the Taliban in killing and wounding Americans in Afghanistan. Here was the White House rewarding this terror regime by legitimizing its nuclear weapons program. Sound familiar?

TURKEY AND ANOTHER CIA DIRECTOR WHO LOST THE PLOT

Because of my years in combat in Middle Eastern theaters, I was focused on that region and how it affected US interests. It wasn't surprising that given my experience, some of the people who approached the Flynn Intel Group with projects were from that region. One was a Turkish businessman named Ekim Alptekin. He wanted help building the image of the Turkish business community in America.

I've never had the pleasure of visiting Turkey, but I've spent a great deal of time with my Turkish counterparts in different assignments over many years, and I respect the Turks a great deal. I had a great working relationship with the Turkish military during my time in Afghanistan as the senior intelligence officer for the International Security Assistance Force and as the senior intelligence officer for the Joint Special Operations Command. The Turks operated out in a very dangerous part of Afghanistan, Regional Command West. RCW bordered with Iran, and the Turkish forces there could speak Farsi. I found the Turkish military to be quite professional, and their leaders were very straightforward. When I traveled out to western Afghanistan to visit them, I would do it to check on the situation in their region and what they were seeing along the Iranian border. I held them in high regard, as they did me.

Anyway, Flynn Intel Group had a good relationship with Ekim. My business partner Bijan Kian (sometimes referred to as Bijan Rafiekian) was the principal for this project. He had a previous relationship with Ekim, from past business. Ekim was always straightforward, and he has a sharp mind. He was also clearly connected to leadership in the Turkish government. But contrary to the claims later made against us, in an effort to implicate me in another fake scandal, we were never paid by the Turkish government. All the money for the project came directly from Ekim's business. The DOJ later admitted this during the course of their prosecution of me.

PFC Charles Flynn (father)
Fort Dix, NJ
October 1943

Charles and Helen Flynn
(mother and father)
Michael Flynn's Parents
On their honeymoon in New York City
May 1946

George and Pat Andrade
(Lori's parents)
Wedding
Newport, RI
June 4th, 1955

Michael Flynn
Middletown High School Islanders
Middletown, RI
Captain & Linebacker
1976

Michael and Lori (wife) Flynn
Wedding
Portsmouth, Rhode Island
1981

Michael Flynn
Ranger School Graduation
Georgia
1982

Helen (mother) and Michael Flynn
Family Wedding
Boston, MA
2012

Michael and Thomas (grandson) Flynn
Fort McNair, DC
2012

Michael and Brooke (granddaughter) Flynn
2012

Michael and Lori (wife) Flynn
Incoming Change of Command into DIA
Bolling Air Force Base, MD
2012

Japanese Prime Minister Shinzō Abe met with President-elect
Donald Trump at Trump Tower
November 17th, 2016
Photo Credit: Prime Minister's Office of Japan

Michael and Travis (grandson) Flynn
Newport, Rhode Island
2018

Michael Flynn and Barbara (sister)
The Rock at Surfer's End
Middletown, RI
2018

Michael Flynn
The Rock at Surfer's End
Middletown, RI
2019

Matthew (son), Michael, Lori (wife), and Michael (son) Flynn
Alexandria, VA
2020

Michael (son), Travis (grandson), and Michael Flynn
Sarasota, FL
2021

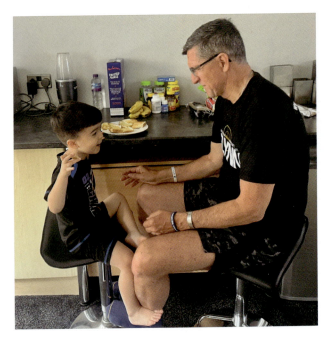

Michael and John (grandson) Flynn
Vacation in England
2024

So we did a strategic assessment of the Turkish business community's reputation in the United States, and one of the things we focused on was this character, Fethullah Gülen. He was a Turkish Muslim leader who came to the US in 1999 and lived here until his death in October 2024 in a big retreat in the Pocono Mountains. He had numerous business interests in the US, most of which seem to be in education. He had a lot of schools around the country that teach Islam and imports foreigners to teach. As we discovered, his hundreds of charter schools are funded by US taxpayers and have been granted more H1-B visas than Google. The more we dug into him, the more it seemed he was a nefarious character with ties inside the US government, mainly in the intelligence community.[17]

The Turkish government, and many Turks, also believe that Gülen played a role in planning the failed coup attempt in 2016 that tried to topple the Ankara government.[18] And that also became part of our research. It struck me that Gülen was operating within the United States in ways that appeared to be irregular and dangerous, to say the least.

This seemed like a potential problem for the United States. Turkey is a NATO member, and whether we like the leadership or not, we have a responsibility to deal with them. We also have long-standing ties in other ways with the Turkish government as well as the Turkish people, and it's our responsibility to live up to our obligations.

One further note about this project. After I left the White House in 2017, there were reports that Ekim and I had met at lunch to hatch a plan to kidnap Gülen and send him back to Turkey. The story was another stupid fantasy—this time sourced to former CIA director James Woolsey. But like so many other so-called "reports," this was nothing more than fodder fed to the left-wing mobs to attack me.

---

17 Congressional Research Service, "Fethullah Gulen, Turkey, and the United States: A Reference," updated April 10, 2017, 2–3, https://crsreports.congress.gov/product/pdf/IF/IF10444/4.
18 CRS, 1.

There was no lunch; it was a very late evening meeting that Ekim and Bijan had set up with a visiting Turkish delegation attending an international conference in New York City. The meeting occurred prior to the November election. It was fully investigated by the DOJ and the FBI, and they found nothing wrong with the meeting. I had been in NYC traveling with the Trump campaign. The meeting was a meet and greet. There was no discussion of Gülen in the meeting at all. Nothing substantive was discussed other than we saw Turkey as an ally, and we appreciated their time. I believe the meeting was more for Ekim to show his Turkish friends that he had secured a serious American client, the Flynn Intel Group, and it was made up of serious people, like me, a former DIA director, and a former CIA director, James Woolsey.

But Woolsey wasn't serious. He arrived a bit late, and he appeared to have spilled something on his crotch. I didn't know him well. He and I had met and spoken at different events. But Bijan had a long-standing relationship with him and brought him into this project. Woolsey's later characterization of this meeting was completely distorted. By the time he'd told this story, it was clear that he'd gone off the deep end. When it came out, I was shocked. Maybe I shouldn't have been—it was another former CIA director lying about something that could have damaged American interests.

MEETING TRUMP

At the same time, I was doing media and other speaking appearances, I was briefing presidential candidates to talk to them about the threats we faced and the weaponization of the intelligence community. There was Carly Fiorina, who was terrific and very smart. Also, Senator Ted Cruz, Wisconsin Governor Scott Walker, and Dr. Ben Carson. They all asked good questions. I met with all of them multiple times except for Walker. I did a long Skype interview with him. I liked him too. I studied up on them before I spoke with them because I didn't know them beforehand, except for Senator Cruz, for whom I have a lot of respect.

The main point I wanted to make to all of them was that we have to get out of the wars we're in. From my perspective coming out of the military and senior positions in the intelligence community is that we can set the conditions for a stronger country if we can end these wars and stop pouring trillions of dollars into foreign military adventures that we're not winning. I was looking for anybody who wanted to have that kind of conversation.

The fifth candidate I spoke with was Donald Trump. I got a call from his campaign team in August 2015 asking me to come to New York to meet the candidate. I flew into New York and then drove to Trump Tower. I arrived half an hour early, and Corey Lewandowski met me in his office. He was Trump's campaign manager at the time. He explained that the candidate had been watching and listening to me and appreciated some of the things that I was saying and wanted to meet. He told me I would have about thirty minutes with him.

I ended up waiting another forty-five minutes and was thinking, *Okay, this is probably going to be a quick five-minute meet and greet. Maybe I've wasted my time.* Then Corey called me in to meet with the candidate, and we ended up speaking for about two hours. I realized his view of the world was very broad. We started to talk about the Middle East and our wars there, but then we covered the entire world. He was interested in the fact that we were constantly at war and how we needed to figure out ways to escape these wars. I was surprised by that and pleased. I emphasized that I wasn't anti-war, but I was against the stupid wars we keep getting ourselves into.

Of course, he also wanted to talk about China. He said that China was ripping us off and Russia was a different case. He had an idea to draw Russia away from China, which made sense to me. At the time, Russia was not a threat to us, and China clearly was. I'd seen how we and the Russians shared a mutual interest in fighting radical Islam, and I believed there were other things we could work on together, maybe even China. He also believed that the US and NATO had screwed up—rather than trying to strengthen the relationship with Moscow, we'd antagonized the Russians. Trump strongly believed he could strengthen ties with Russia, and I fully supported that.

Before I left, he wanted me to meet his son Eric, and I thought that was very nice of him to introduce me to a family member. It was a genuinely human thing to do. Eric's a good-looking, extremely intelligent, and tall young man, and we chatted for a few minutes. Then I was ready to leave and told Trump it was great meeting him, and he should let me know how I could help in the future. I continued to advise him as well as Cruz. I liked what I heard from the two of them about their plans for the country.

I remember in February 2016 telling my brother Joe that the only person who can beat Hillary Clinton is Donald Trump. He looked at me and said, "Donald Trump, are you out of your mind?" I told him that the country was ready for something different. The country needed something different, and if we didn't get it, there were going to be bigger problems headed our way.

I'd met Hillary Clinton before. She was in a committee hearing where I testified. She's smart, and she has a skill set. But the problems with her were clear to me.

To start with, there was her using a private email server to conduct government business. I spent ten years as an electronic warfare and signals intelligence officer. I also have a master's degree in telecommunications, so I clearly know the damage she did as secretary of state by using an unclassified server to conduct official business. She did real harm to the country and refused to accept any responsibility or accountability for mishandling highly classified information. If anyone else, including me or any of the intelligence officers who had worked for me, had played that loosely with American secrets they'd be looking at jail time. As far as I was concerned, no one who'd ever held a security clearance could support her.

And her failure to take responsibility for the server stood for an even bigger issue—her lack of accountability in general. It shows her contempt for our laws and, more importantly, our principles, the things that hold us together as Americans. It means she's contemptuous of the American people. And it's not like she's ever hidden it. She shows it in the way she treats people and talks about people, the Americans who she thinks are beneath her. Her comment on the campaign trail about Trump supporters being "deplorables" is only the most famous example of how she's contemptuous of the "little people," but she's also proud of it.

And that's why people like her go into government. Service is the furthest thing from their minds. They work the machinery of the federal government to take power and control for themselves and away from We the People. Of course, it's not just her; it's most of them, Republicans as well as Democrats. They may have differences of opinion about illegal immigration, and the size of government, bigger or smaller, higher or lower taxes, and so on, but underneath, they're the same. And Hillary Clinton stands for them all—she's like the poster child for political greed and corruption.

Trump was coming at this from the other direction. He didn't need the money. He said he loved America, and we connected on that. When I signed on with Donald J. Trump, my life changed, and in ways I couldn't possibly have imagined.

CHAPTER 7

ON THE CAMPAIGN

BARNSTORMING WITH TRUMP

The word "campaign" is originally a military term referring to an operation in a particular locale for a period of time. For instance, one of the most famous campaigns in history is the Normandy Campaign, which started with D-Day, on June 6, 1944, and lasted until July 24, 1944. Obviously, there's no combat in political campaigns, no casualties, and no bloodshed, but with Donald J. Trump running for president, the team had a very real sense we were embarking on a campaign to preserve our great country.

It gave me the opportunity to travel around our great country and meet Americans from every walk of life. It reinforced what I believed about America—a nation blessed by God and filled with remarkable people from coast to coast. And what became clearer than ever meeting those Americans is that our country was hurting. Our two failed foreign wars and the jobs sacrificed when the corporate elites moved our manufacturing base to Mexico and China were responsible for what Trump called "American carnage."

Voters had no faith in their political elites, and why should they? Democrats and Republicans had sold them out time and again. It's as if they'd forgotten that they governed on behalf of the voters who hired them and cared only about pleasing the donors who made their campaigns possible. So when Trump came along, they heard a wealthy celebrity of all people singing their song. Being on the campaign trail with Donald J. Trump was a life-changing experience.

I got to know the candidate fairly well. He and I shared opinions about people, the media, and ideas about things to do once he won. He knew he had to deal with the political people around him, and many he didn't care for at all. But for him to get around the country, he had to rely on state Republican chairs, and he knew he needed to rely on people like Reince Priebus, then the chair of the Republican National Committee.

But he also had allies in his inner circle, like Steve Bannon and Kellyanne Conway, and especially his family, his children Don Jr., Eric, and Ivanka, and his son-in-law Jared Kushner. During those intense days, weeks, and months, we spent many hours together.

I saw Trump the strategic thinker speaking to large and small audiences about the details of foreign policy issues, the dangers of nuclear war, the nation's failing energy policies, and the advantages and disadvantages of organizations like NATO and the United Nations. Trump is not only an exceptional businessman, but his strategic sense of the global and American landscapes comes from a broad range of international experiences over his storied life. He may have spent a lot of time on his show, *The Apprentice*, or traveling around checking on his numerous properties, but what I witnessed was a man who was a voracious reader of everything. He read extensively on every trip we went on together. Whether it was the global affairs section, or op-eds, or even the sports pages, Trump was on top of the numerous issues you would expect from a CEO who owns a global company. He was, without a doubt, always well-informed. He relied on people who were experts to give him advice, and he routinely sought advice. There were people in his orbit who had broad experiences in all sorts of areas. Another of his rare talents is his unlimited energy. As I got to know him better, he and I would talk about our parents. Without a doubt, Trump attributes his success to both his parents. He doesn't drink or smoke. He has never smoked. His parents lived into their nineties and my sense is that Trump will do the same if the Deep State doesn't eliminate him first.

I also saw him as a strong family man, something the media lies about constantly or simply refuses to discuss. Even his ex-wives don't have anything bad to say about him. And he clearly loves his children. On the campaign trail, I also had the opportunity to meet with Melania, who is one of the nicest people I've ever met. During the

New York City town hall event with Trump and Clinton aboard the USS *Intrepid* in September (the one where Donna Brazile provided crooked Hillary Clinton with the questions beforehand, I sat next to Melania.)[19] We were just exchanging small talk, but it was one of those unforgettable moments because she was such a class act at a moment when the media was starting to really show its hatred of Trump.

There were mostly veterans in the audience on board the *Intrepid* that night. The moderators wanted to talk about Russia, like all the media that summer and fall. They asked Trump about Putin, and he compared him to Obama. The Russian president, Trump said, "has very strong control over a country." He said Russia's system is very different from ours, "and I don't happen to like the system, but certainly in that system, he's been a leader. Far more than our president has been a leader." Unfortunately for America, Trump couldn't have been more right, and the vets in the audience knew it as well as I did. Putin had Obama wrapped around his little finger.

For just one example, when Obama walked back his redline threatening to take action against Bashar al-Assad for using chemical weapons against his own people, Putin came to Obama's rescue. He promised to confiscate the Syrian regime's unconventional arsenal, but everyone knows that if you have the right components, it's easy to rebuild a chemical weapons arsenal in no time.

I'm not saying Obama should have pushed US troops into the Syrian war, only that when you draw redlines, you're putting American prestige on the line. Obama showed weakness, and Putin highlighted it.

I flew with Trump around the country for lots of campaign events. I was on the stage introducing the candidate the night he was speaking to the African American community in Michigan and asked them for their vote—"What do you have to lose?" he said. It was totally unscripted. He had, and has, a great group of speechwriters,

---

19 Aidan Quigley, "Brazile: Leaking Town Hall Topics to Clinton Campaign 'Mistake I Will Forever Regret,'" *POLITICO*, March 17, 2017, https://www.politico.com/story/2017/03/donna-brazile-hillary-clinton-leak-regret-236184.

but the most memorable stuff he said was always his, and usually off-the-cuff, like this was. He knew that the Black community knew the truth—that the Democrats didn't really care about them, not even Obama, the first "African-American" president. The Democrats had already proven that things weren't going to get better for Black people by voting with the Democrats, so why not give him a shot at improving black lives? Like he said, "What do you have to lose?"

I was with him when he spontaneously decided to go do a rally out in Grand Junction, Colorado, before heading to Denver. He tweeted that we were going to be in Grand Junction the next day, and we laughed and thought maybe we'll get a few thousand to show up to a rally at this airport in the middle of nowhere. When we arrived, the hangar and the entire airfield were packed. Well, over 10,000 supporters showed up.

"This is incredible," he told the crowd. "You know we have people wrapped all the way around the hangar." Trump continued: "We're going to deliver real, real change. It's going to be a beautiful thing, and we are going to end the government of corruption, which it has definitely been. And we are going to drain the swamp in Washington, D.C., and that's what it is."

It's amazing when I look back at that speech and all the problems that Trump identified. He promised he was going to fix them, and he did, or at least started to repair them. And now Biden has set us back to square one, or worse.

"We're also going to renegotiate our terrible trade deals," Trump said that night. "End illegal immigration, stop the massive inflow of refugees, reduce surging crime all over our country, cut taxes and regulations."

Trump loves our military, and part of what I discussed with him is that it was in bad shape. I'd just published a book in July called *The Field of Fight: How We Win the Global War Against Radical Islam and Its Allies* explaining what we'd gotten wrong in Iraq and Afghanistan and what we needed to get right to defeat an adversary determined to destroy us. Waging two wars for a decade and a half at that stage and not winning them will deplete and demoralize a military.

And that night in Grand Junction, Trump promised to rebuild it. "We have the greatest people in the world in our military," he said, "but it has really become depleted, and we are going to fix it and make it better, and hopefully never have to use it. But it's going to be there."

And then he called on me and General Keith Kellogg, who was also with the campaign. "You guys are great," he said as he waved us on stage. There is a good picture of Trump and me on the stage. "I just spoke to the generals," Trump said, gesturing toward us. "These are real generals too. These are real guys. I love having them on my plane, but when I'm on my plane with them I sort of feel like I'm number three. Does that make sense? You know, they're generals."

Just the day before, news had broken about retired Marine General James Cartwright. He'd been under investigation for leaking classified information to a journalist about the Iran nuclear program. Cartwright said he didn't, and he was never charged for it, but he was charged with lying to the FBI.[20] Both Keith and I knew Cartwright. Trump asked me on stage why Cartwright was being held accountable, but Clinton wasn't. I said on stage that Cartwright "took responsibility and accountability for his actions. She did not, and she deserves—he did a tenth of what she did, and he's going to find himself probably serving a jail sentence. And Hillary Clinton did exactly the same, lied to the FBI, under oath. Unbelievable."

Eventually, Cartwright was pardoned by Obama, but that didn't change the basic point. There was a lack of accountability in our government, and Clinton was the worst. And Clinton's corruption was one of my big messages on the campaign trail. In fact, that's how the famous "lock her up" chant started at the Republican National Convention in mid-July.

---

20 Department of Justice, Office of Public Affairs, "Former Vice Chairman of the Joint Chiefs of Staff Pleads Guilty to Federal Felony in Leak Investigation," press release, October 17, 2016, https://www.justice.gov/opa/pr/former-vice-chairman-joint-chiefs-staff-pleads-guilty-federal-felony-leak-investigation#:~:text=All%20News-,Former%20Vice%20Chairman%20of%20the%20Joint%20Chiefs%20of%20Staff%20Pleads,Federal%20Felony%20in%20Leak%20Investigation&text=Retired%20General%20James%20E.,unauthorized%20disclosure%20of%20classified%20information.

In my speech, I said, "We do not need a reckless President who believes she is above the law." The audience started to chant "Lock her up, lock her up." I heard them, and I responded, "Lock her up. That's right, yep that's right. Lock her up."

Looking back, maybe I should have stepped back and just let the audience chant their hearts out. They were emotionally charged, I was emotionally charged, and the moment got away from me.

Sometimes I wish I had that moment back. But the fact is, she should have been locked up or otherwise held accountable for her actions. The audience was right. They know how representative government is supposed to work—government by, for, and of the people.

Trump won over the American people because he promised to restore the principles of our way of government and return the power to the people "We're going to win," he said that night at Grand Junction. "We're going to take back the White House, we're going to put America first again."

FIRST EVIDENCE OF RUSSIAGATE

All summer press reports were speculating on Donald Trump's ties to Russia. During the Democratic National Committee, there was a leak of DNC emails allegedly hacked by the Russians. Or at least that what's the Clinton campaign claimed—based only on information provided by a Clinton campaign contractor called CrowdStrike that specialized in cybersecurity. CrowdStrike never shared the DNC servers with the FBI or any other agency—and as it later turned out, even CrowdStrike said there was no conclusive evidence that the Russians, or anyone for that matter, had ever stolen DNC emails. But at the time, the Clintons and their media allies said the Russians had leaked those stolen emails to help Trump.

I remember that people from the Trump campaign asked the candidate if he had Russian connections, and Trump had no idea what they were talking about. Neither did I, because I was certain he didn't. As an intelligence officer, there are different things you notice about people who have problems like that with foreign countries—we had a few cases like that at DIA and resolved them quickly. No way was there anything going on with the candidate and the Russians—I spent so much time with him that I'd have been the first to know.

Also I knew more than enough about the FBI to recognize that if one of the world's biggest celebrities—a Manhattan real estate magnate and TV star—had connections with Russian organized crime or Russian officials, the bureau would have had a thick file on it from his time in New York, where they have a very large field office. And as a former director of a US intelligence agency, I'd have been given a defensive briefing on it, especially when it was clear I was spending time with the campaign.

Nonetheless, I thought it was a good idea to set the record straight. After all, part of what was fueling all the talk about the Trump team's ties to Russia was my appearance at the RT dinner in December 2015. So, I did an interview with *The Washington Post* that was published on August 15.

The interviewer asked why I'd appeared on RT, and I said I'd been on Al Jazeera, Sky News Arabia, CNN, Fox, MSNBC, and so on. The interviewer said that RT was state-run, and I rolled my eyes. Like CNN and MSNBC weren't messaging on behalf of a political body—the Democrat Party.

I explained that one of the reasons I went was because Russia had lost respect for us. "If I have any sort of fiber in my body where I can help out to make sure they understand that we have people in our country who aren't going to apologize for who we are," I said. "We're not going to act in a soft way for what we believe needs to be done."

I said I learned on that trip that Putin had no respect for US leadership under Obama. "I just learned it from the conversations and the way questions were asked and the discussions I was part of," I told the *Post*. "I'm arguing for the United States, and I found myself with people wondering what's going on with the U.S. and I would tell them, you know, of course I'm standing up for the U.S. But it's hard when they don't have any respect for the current leadership."

Not surprisingly, the interviewer brought it back around to the allegations that the *Post* and other media had been making all summer about Trump advisers and Russia. He asked about business ties between Russia and Trump team members Carter Page and Paul Manafort. I said I didn't know anything about that—but I did know something about the Clintons and their financial arrangements with foreign powers. "Look at the amount of money the Clinton Global Initiative is taking from countries right now," I said. "It's an incredible level of corruption."

I pointed out the contradictions of Obama's Russia policy. He imposed sanctions on Russia because of its invasion of Crimea, but "at the same time, we're dealing with Russia on Iranian nuclear weapons. So, when people go, Ukraine and Russia are bad, but at the same time we're sitting down with Russia on giving the lead state sponsor of terror [Iran] a pathway to a nuclear bomb."

I concluded by saying that having relations with Russia is important to US interests. "We worked very closely with them on the Sochi Olympics," I said. I pointed out that "we beat Hitler because of our relationship with the Russians"—and that was when Stalin was the power in Moscow. So we could and should have a relationship with Moscow under Putin to support shared interests. I said that we "have a problem with radical Islamism and I actually think that we could work together with them against this enemy."

Who knows if any of those ideas got through to the readers of a newspaper written and read by Democratic Party voters? But at least it was on the record. Of course, what I didn't know at the time was that just the day before, August 14, the FBI had opened an investigation on me—because of my alleged ties to Russia.[21] What evidence

21 *United States of America v. Michael T. Flynn*, United States District Court for the District of Columbia, Case 1:17-cr-00232-EGS, Document 198, p. 28, filed May 7, 2020, https://storage.courtlistener.com/recap/gov.uscourts.dcd.191592/gov.uscourts.dcd.191592.198.0_6.pdf.

did they have? None of course—except the trip to Moscow for the RT dinner, which was known to the highest levels of the defense and intelligence communities at the time.

There were three other Trump aides under investigation: Paul Manafort, then the campaign manager; Carter Page, a business consultant and former Navy officer, whom I'd never met; and someone else I'd never met, George Papadopoulos, a young former Washington, DC, think-tanker. This was the basis for the umbrella investigation called "Crossfire Hurricane." The specific investigation targeting me was "Crossfire Razor."

Here's an important piece that sheds light on the nature of that investigation. Shortly after I left the DIA in September 2014, I went through a full, months-long security clearance background investigation, including taking a polygraph test. By late spring 2015, I had all my clearances updated without any problems. So, what sense does it make that a little more than a year later the FBI suspects I'm a Russian asset? Right, Crossfire Hurricane was never an investigation—it was a political hit-job executed by people and organizations within the Obama administration from the outset.

The reason for opening what the FBI terms a "full investigation" on me and the three others was to move to the next step and get a warrant to collect the campaign's electronic communications, emails, texts, phone calls, and so on. That's why the Clinton campaign and FBI invented the story about Trump and Russia—to get a warrant that specifically targeted foreign intelligence, the Foreign Intelligence Surveillance Act (FISA) warrant, one of the most intrusive surveillance tools in the intelligence community's arsenal.

And the FBI did eventually get a FISA on Carter Page.[22] The evidence used for it was garbage—a collection of fake memos supposedly compiled by a former British intelligence officer, Christopher

---

22 White House, memo from Donald F. McGahn II, Counsel to the President, to Devin Nunes, Chairman, House Permanent Select Committee on Intelligence, February 2, 2018, https://intelligence.house.gov/uploadedfiles/memo_and_white_house_letter.pdf (PAGE 4).

Steele. In reality, the whole story was cooked up by yet another Clinton campaign contractor, a Washington-based communications firm called Fusion GPS. But what started as a political dirty trick was endorsed by the director of the CIA, John Brennan, and the director of the FBI, James Comey, who played a direct role in overseeing the FBI's illegal surveillance of a political campaign. It's not just the CIA and certain FBI agents who went rogue—they were following their rogue directors.

What the FBI really wanted to know had nothing to do with Russia. No, it was whether or not the Trump campaign knew anything about the emails from Clinton's private server—in particular, if we knew whether they'd be dropped before the election as an October surprise to ruin Clinton's candidacy.

Stefan Halper, the Cambridge professor who spread the fake narrative about me being compromised at the Cambridge dinner, was one of the FBI's confidential human sources and approached both Page and Papadopoulos with very specific questions that show what the bureau was looking for—he asked them repeatedly about Clinton's emails and whether they would be leaked as an October surprise to benefit the Trump team.

Halper is one of the most destructive figures in recent American history. He's as bad as all the Watergate plumbers rolled into one, and he did exactly the same thing—he was at the center of a government plot to spy on and disrupt a presidential campaign. Yet unlike Richard Nixon's dirty operatives, Stefan Halper has never paid the price for his crimes and maybe never will, but in my opinion, he should.[23]

GOP ESTABLISHMENT SHOWS TRUE COLORS

As it happened, the Trump campaign had to deal with its own October surprise—though it's still unclear who was behind it, the Clinton

---

23 Margot Cleveland, "SCOOP: CIA, FBI Informant Was *Washington Post* Source for Russiagate Smears," *The Federalist*, November 4, 2019, https://thefederalist.com/2019/11/04/scoop-cia-fbi-informant-was-washington-post-source-for-russiagate-smears/.

campaign or the Republican establishment. Circumstantial evidence suggests it may have been an inside job. Here's the inside story.

Earlier in the summer, I got a phone call from then-campaign manager Corey Lewandowski notifying me that the campaign was vetting me for the vice presidential nomination. I hadn't expected that at all—the number two spot on the ticket. He said that they needed some information for a background check. I had a packet ready to give him for vetting because, as I explained above, my clearances had just been renewed.

There's a famous picture of me and the three other people who were reportedly in the running for the vice presidential slot: me, Newt Gingrich, Chris Christie, and Mike Pence. It was pretty humbling just to be in the running for a job like that. My family could barely believe it. What was interesting about the photo is that three of the men were hard-core, establishment Republicans and one was a registered Democrat, me. And when Trump called me just before the Republican National Convention in mid-July to tell me he was going with Pence, he joked that was the reason why.

I was at home in Alexandria, Virginia, with Lori when I got a phone call from the candidate. It was a really informal call, casual, like two friends speaking. He said, "Well, you know, I'm not going to go with you as the vice president." He told me he was on his way to Indiana, and Mike Pence was going to be his choice. He said, "Maybe at another time, but you know, you're a Democrat." I laughed and said, "No problem. I'm here to help however I can. I just appreciate everything and let me know what you want me to do, and I'll help you out."

Maybe I should've been more disappointed, but it was a really memorable call. He was great to me and always treated me with respect. He called me Mike in private, sometimes, but always referred to me as "General" in public. He asked me to call him Donald, and I did—until he became the commander-in-chief. Then I called him Mr. President.

He almost didn't win because people on our own team were trying to undermine him. It was during his debates with Clinton that I realized the Republican establishment didn't want him to win. Even Reince Priebus and Mike Pence indicated they thought Trump had no chance in these debates. They didn't like the way he prepared, nor did they appreciate his sense of what the American people wanted. Trump knew America needed a massive change, and the GOP wanted to keep things going as is.

Chris Christie was on some of the campaign trips—what a horse's ass. He has a big mouth and always wanted to be the center of attention. He hated the fact that Trump was the candidate and not him. He and Trump had a long-term relationship, but I didn't see what it was built on, except that Christie needed attention.

Rudy Giuliani on the other hand was a loyal and trusted friend to Trump. He stuck up for him on every occasion—not like a needy hanger-on, but like a true friend to the candidate. And Rudy and Trump's insider New York stories always cracked me up. I remember flying with them on Trump's private plane and Rudy relating stories about how corrupt Hillary really was. We all had our own perspectives on her, but all agreed. It's just amazing what she was able to get away with her whole political career.

And then in the first week of October, here comes the October surprise—it's the infamous *Access Hollywood* video from 2005 where Trump talks about how women are attracted to celebrities, like him. What stuck was an ugly phrase the candidate used that I'm sure I don't have to repeat as it got so much attention at the time. I didn't like to hear it, but I also thought it was ridiculous Trump was being strung up for something he told another man in private more than a decade before. As I say, I thought it was ugly, but to be honest I've heard much worse and every guy has, which is why that October surprise fell flat.

Except with some big-name Republicans who came out immediately to denounce Trump. It was a pile-on from the right, which is why we were pretty confident the tape had been leaked by the GOP to sabotage the campaign.

I was told that Pence and Priebus had prepared resignation letters if it got really bad for Trump. I didn't find this surprising because my interactions with both were always uncomfortable. Neither was ever truly loyal to Trump.

What did surprise me was that, according to what several campaign aides told me, Pence was also prepared to accept the nomination for president if Trump decided to walk away from the campaign. It seems that from the beginning some of the political operatives were just waiting for Trump to give up and say, "Screw this, I don't need this political stuff, I'm going to go back to being a real estate magnate, a great businessman, and run the beautiful companies that I have." Their hope, their fantasy, was that Trump would turn tail, Pence would take over, and Paul Ryan become the vice presidential candidate, again, just like he was with Mitt Romney's failed 2012 run for the White House.

You might remember that some of the Republican establishment was committed to the idea of pushing Trump out throughout his presidency, like when they started to discuss invoking the Twenty-Fifth Amendment to remove him from office, soon after he moved into the Oval Office.

I never felt comfortable around Pence. Lastly, on occasion, Trump was known to use the f-bomb here and there. I witnessed on a few occasions when we were together with Pence, Trump would say, "Mike hates it when I use the F word." Pence would simply stand there with a dumb smirk on his face and say nothing.

ELECTION DAY

I had to vote in Virginia, and I wanted to vote in person with my wife. We had never voted together due to my many deployments— and my staying out of politics as a military officer. The fact is, in my thirty-three years in the military, I never once voted for president of the United States. Nor did I ever vote at a normal voting booth; it was always by military absentee ballot. I felt it was not my place to vote for who my commander-in-chief was supposed to be. I stayed out of politics and instead focused on my military mission. However, this time, I had decided to stay at home and vote, and then Lori and I would watch the results come in at home, and I would stay in touch with Trump and the campaign team up in New York.

I'd have enjoyed being at election headquarters that night because I had worked hard for a Trump victory. I felt I'd brought in a lot of votes, including the overwhelming support from veterans. But I wanted to be at home with my wife. We had already spent so much time apart, so being with her was clearly the right move. During Trump's acceptance speech that night, he called my name out from the stage, and I always appreciated that he did that. He clearly recognized the role I played helping him get elected as POTUS.

Once key states started to fall toward him, especially North Carolina, I knew he would be the next POTUS. At about 8:00 p.m., I called Trump to tell him I thought he was going to win and to get ready. It was a brief call, and his response was, "Thank you, General, we're going to do great things together."

And when he was officially announced as the victor, I reserved a train ticket up to New York to prepare for the next stages of the Trump presidency. He'd defeated the establishment, first the Republicans, then the Democrats. All the momentum was going our way.

The next stage was the transition, from the Obama administration to the Trump administration. The outgoing president said that his White House would do everything to effect a smooth transition, but nothing could have been further from the truth. I've described this transition as war. From November 9, the day after the election, to Inauguration Day, January 20, we fought every single day with our predecessors even to accomplish simple tasks. And they laid traps for us all throughout the government that the new president would wind up fighting for four years. Obama's subterfuges were designed to preserve his legacy and destroy his successor.

CHAPTER 8

A TRANSITION LIKE WAR

ME AND KIM JONG-UN?

After the election, Donald Trump immediately began staffing his administration. The first person he asked to join was Republican National Committee chairman, Reince Priebus, as the chief of staff. At the time, it made sense because as Republican National Committee chair, Priebus knew lots of people who could fill important roles in the new administration. The second person the president-elect chose to serve in his administration was me. It came about in an interesting way.

I was asked what position I wanted by members of his family and by other close advisers and instead, I said I wanted to help give names to fill the administration with good people. And I was asked again, "But what job do you want?" I said that I didn't really want anything. That's not why I campaigned for him. I did it because I wanted to see the country go in a different direction. I stood up for him and I stood up with him, and we won.

On November 10, two days after the election, the president-elect went to the Oval Office for a meeting with the outgoing president. It's traditional for the two to meet, almost like a low-key ceremony to celebrate the peaceful transfer of power. The presidents talk about the country, the world, and the government—in a low-key meeting that signals the beginning of the transition process, from one administration to the next.

"I want to emphasize to you, Mr. President-elect," Barack Obama said to Trump, "that we now are going to want to do everything we can to help you succeed because if you succeed, then the country succeeds." But of course, nothing could have been further from the truth. Then-President Obama was lying straight to the face of the incoming and duly elected president, Donald J. Trump. No one in US history had ever interfered with the peaceful transition of power like Obama would over the next three months.

The sitting president set traps throughout the bureaucracies wherever he could, and naturally, the media played along. It wasn't just the partisan stories they published—we expected that. We knew the media hated Trump, and they hated all of us. And we knew the press corps had never been so beholden to a president as they were to Obama. They said there were no scandals during his eight years in office, but that was a lie—the media just buried them. I knew because I was a casualty of one of Obama's cover-ups. I'd told the truth about al-Qaeda and ISIS and how they posed a threat to our national security. But that was an inconvenient truth that crossed up the political narrative, so I was out, buried.

But what the media embarked on with the transition process was something else again—they served as the platform for an information operation that was devised to delegitimize a president and thereby destabilize the country that elected him. Through a seemingly endless series of leaks of classified information, the press coordinated with rogue elements of the intelligence services to push the Russiagate narrative on the American public. That was all accomplished with Obama at the helm.

A few days after they met, I was up in New York City at Trump Tower and got a call from Trump's secretary. She said that the president-elect wanted to speak with me. So I went upstairs, and he debriefed me on his meeting with Obama. He said Obama warned him about two people—Kim Jong-un, the North Korean dictator, and me.[24] The former was definitely a threat to American peace and prosperity, but me? I couldn't believe it.

---

24 "Hope Hicks Interview," Committee on the Judiciary, US House of Representatives, June 19, 2019, p.191, https://www.justsecurity.org/wp-content/uploads/2019/08/Transcript-Judiciary-Committee-Interview-of-Hope-Hicks.pdf.

Trump asked me what I thought. I said that I've never met Barack Obama, although he picked me twice for two key jobs. Trump asked, why would he say something like that? I said I had no idea. Then the president-elect said, "Neither do I." He said that he didn't trust the guy. We were standing there for a few seconds, and then he said, "I want you to come in as my national security advisor."

The staff laughed when they heard about Obama warning Trump about me. I didn't understand why Obama would feel so threatened by me. Maybe he was leaving an early clue as to what he was setting in motion to disrupt the administration—and the stability of the country. Of course, no one knew at the time that the FBI had a FISA warrant on a Trump aide that would allow them to sweep up the communications of all the Trump circle, including Trump himself. [25] At the same time, dozens of Obama officials, all the way up to then Vice President Joe Biden, would soon have the transition team under surveillance.

But on November 18, the president-elect officially named me his national security advisor. Lori and I had talked about it, and she already knew that if asked, I would gladly honor the incoming president's request. We talked about what it meant after thirty-three years in the Army—that we were starting on another journey along the path we'd walked for more than three decades, service to the country.

It was an exciting time for the country. Everything felt new again, and at the same time, we were going to restore the values and principles that made our country great from its founding—a government built to serve the people and help them fulfill their dreams. I'd be working for a guy who wasn't a politician but someone who stepped up when his country needed someone from the outside to speak the truth and help fix America.

We were going to raise the country again because we were in a tough spot. We're losing two wars and running counterterrorism oper-

---

25 John Solomon, "Memos Detail FBI's 'Hurry the F Up Pressure' to Probe Trump Campaign," *The Hill*, July 6, 2018, https://thehill.com/hilltv/rising/395776-memos-detail-fbis-hurry-the-f-up-pressure-to-probe-trump-campaign/.

ations around the world. The economy wasn't great. And more than half the electorate believed we were moving in the wrong direction. As the national security advisor, I would have a role in all those areas, impacting and influencing the decisions of the president and helping improve the lives of Americans. To boil it down, my job was to help keep the government honest, authentic, and transparent in its efforts to serve those who make America great—the American people.

HIT THE GROUND RUNNING

The national security advisor is the president's principal advisor on all national security issues. I'd held two Senate-confirmed positions in the Obama administration, but the NSA is not a Senate-confirmed position. That means, among other things, you don't have to worry about being loved by the Beltway mob, which doesn't care about the American people anyway. You answer to the president, who was elected by the American people.

It's one of the most powerful positions in the US government because the NSA works out of the White House, advises the president on a daily basis, and travels with him. With regular access to the commander-in-chief, the NSA is independent of the various bureaucracies in the executive branch, like the Departments of Defense, State, Treasury, and so on, as well as the CIA, FBI, and Department of Homeland Security.

The NSA is supported by the National Security Council (NSC) staff, which works out of the Old Executive Office Building, adjoining the White House. Much of the NSC staff is detailed from other agencies to man the numerous desks, covering everything from foreign policy and intelligence to technology and economic interests.

The NSC was created by the National Security Act of 1947, a reshuffling of the US government that also created the CIA. In 1949, the NSC became part of the Executive Office of the President with an executive secretary in charge. That job eventually acquired the title of national security advisor.

John F. Kennedy's NSA, McGeorge Bundy, was a former military intelligence officer who served in World War II. He became famous but for the wrong reasons—he was one of the architects of the Vietnam War. But the post really gained prestige during the Richard Nixon administration when Henry Kissinger held the job for all of Nixon's first term and into his second before the president resigned. Kissinger also served for a time under Nixon's replacement, Gerald Ford.

In the 1980s, at the height of the Cold War, there were 45 people on the NSC staff. When I took it over, there were almost 500 people working for Obama's NSA, Susan Rice. I've led organizations consisting of 20 people all the way up to 20,000, so large staffs and organizations are not unfamiliar turf for me. But the size of the NSC staff, which really started to expand during the George W. Bush administration and exploded under Obama, was not conducive to producing good work—or team-building. Having 500 people on the NSC staff means that at least half don't know what the other half is doing.

My plan was to cut that staff back to 25 people and when needed to pull in experts from elsewhere in the government or even tap civilians for their expertise. One of the best parts of the job is that you have access to virtually anyone you want and can draw on the amazing talents of Americans across the country.

The point was to keep the NSC staff lean in order to do the essential work that the president counted on. Further, as I knew too well from my time in Washington, many of those staffers detailed from other agencies were used to spy on the White House on behalf of their home agencies. I was eliminated before I could root out most of the internal spies.

The result was that one NSC staffer, a CIA official named Eric Ciaramella, weaponized intelligence that was used against Trump.[26] Ciaramella was the famous fake whistleblower who instigated the

---

26   Paul Sperry, RealClearWire, "Impeachment 'Whistleblower' Was in the Loop of Biden-Ukraine Affairs," *Highland County Press*, April 18, 2024, https://highlandcountypress.com/opinions/impeachment-whistleblower-was-loop-biden-ukraine-affairs#gsc.tab=0.

impeachment proceedings against the president because of a phone call between the president and his Ukrainian counterpart. Another NSC staffer named Alexander Vindman had listened in on Trump's call, took the information to Ciaramella, and they were off to the races. Aided by rogue elements of the intelligence community as well as the media and Democratic operatives, these NSC staffers Ciaramella and Vindman ran an operation against the president that did great harm to the country.[27]

Some of the people I brought in, like Matt Pottinger, coauthor of *Fixing Intel*, stayed on after I left and did terrific work on China. Others I hired, like Adam Lovinger, were blocked by the Deep State. Adam was working in the Pentagon's Office of Net Assessment (ONA) at the time, the same office that paid Stefan Halper millions of dollars for his subpar research papers.[28] When Adam started asking why Halper was getting paid so much for lousy academic work, his superiors went after him. Little did I know at the time that Halper, the man they called the Walrus, was going to loom even larger in my life in the months and years to come.

NATIONAL PRIORITIES

Our first priority was to come in steady, look at the big picture, and see what's happening in the world. There were so many pieces already in play, so much raw data, we wanted to see the geostrategic landscape as a whole. The emphasis was going to be using economic instruments since that was the new president's strength and America still had the potential to be the most powerful economy in world history. We were certainly not looking for more conflict. We were working on ways to extricate ourselves from places and stop fighting losing wars.

27 Paul Sperry, "Whistleblower Was Overheard in '17 Discussing with Ally How to Remove Trump," RealClearInvestigations, January 22, 2020, https://www.realclearinvestigations.com/articles/2020/01/22/whistleblower_was_overheard_in_17_discussing_with_ally_how_to_remove_trump_121701.html.

28 Bill Gertz, "Pentagon Pulls Security Clearance of Trump White House Aide," Washington Free Beacon, May 4, 2017, https://freebeacon.com/national-security/pentagon-pulls-security-clearance-trump-white-house-aide/.

The president-elect had talked about China on the campaign trail a lot, and he was right to be worried. By offshoring our manufacturing base to China, our political and corporate establishment had not only added to our trade deficit but had also turned Beijing into an emerging superpower. I'd been stationed in the Pacific in the late eighties into the early nineties, and I saw the rise of China from up close.

While at DIA, I made China my agency's number-one priority and hired the nation's top intelligence analyst as well as a Senior Intelligence Service executive to lead our massive analytic bureau. China is a formidable adversary. I witnessed it throughout my career and was always raising it as our top national security issue even when we were going blow for blow with al-Qaeda. Now with Xi Jinping's One Belt One Road Initiative, stretching from the East China Sea to the western nations of Africa as well as across Europe, this imperial project places China in a vastly stronger geostrategic position.

I even sat down with my NSA predecessor, Susan Rice, five or six times, and my main focus was on China. As DIA director, I had a pretty good sense of what was going on with China, but I wanted to see if there were new developments and most importantly how the outgoing administration had handled them. She couldn't have cared less about China. Her entire focus was on protecting whatever policies she knew we were likely to change, which was all of them. The Obama administration's eight years of failed foreign policy and national security were a disaster and put America into an untenable position globally. I had in mind, along with the direction then-President-elect Trump gave me, to change all of that, but Susan Rice apparently had other nefarious things on her mind.

Russia was also an issue. In 2014, when I was DIA director, Russia invaded Crimea and is still there. There was a significant shooting war still ongoing in eastern Ukraine between Ukrainian forces and pro-Russian separatists that drew in Russian forces—which eventually morphed into full-scale war backed by the Biden administration. At the time, we knew we had to monitor the situation closely, and

I knew Russian strengths and vulnerabilities. I'd been studying the Russians for nearly thirty years.

There was Iran too. Since I'd left the DIA, I'd been warning that the Iran nuclear deal was a terrible mistake, and now we were going to look closely at it. I also wanted a look at the side agreements to the nuclear deal our predecessors had made with Tehran. Those documents weren't classified, but the Obama team had hidden them by mixing them with classified documents. And of course, Iran was still destabilizing the Middle East through its proxies, especially Hezbollah and Hamas.

There was the terror issue too. And unlike the previous administration, we weren't going to imagine away the ISIS threat. I'd laid out the threat clearly in my book *Field of Fight*, and the plan was, as I'd recommended there, to partner with our traditional Sunni partners: Jordan, Egypt, and Saudi Arabia, where Trump would make his first presidential visit in May.

My thirty-three years in the military working in intelligence had prepared me for the NSA job, but I continued to prepare myself. I met with former colleagues. In fact, even before the election, I spoke with former US officials, civilians, and military to get their sense of what threatened our nation. For instance, I met with my former boss General Stanley McChrystal and Admiral William McRaven one night in Virginia. I had worked with both of these officers in Iraq and Afghanistan. They were both quality leaders and, I came to find out, both staunch Democrats. McRaven later said he hadn't supported Clinton after he wrote an op-ed criticizing Trump for stripping John Brennan of his security clearances, but he was full of it. Both McRaven and McChrystal were Clinton supporters—they told me they both had expected big jobs in her White House. McChrystal wanted to be CIA director, and McRaven wanted to be NSA.

Outside of a few brief email exchanges, I haven't heard from either since. They were great and heroic public servants in uniform but in private life became something else. They couldn't see the threats to our nation at home from our corrupt ruling class—or maybe they just wanted to become part of the machine, profiting off their military careers in retirement.

I also spoke with former NSAs, with Henry Kissinger at the top of the list. I met with him three times. I listened and learned, and finally came away disappointed. Kissinger's insights were helpful but outdated, and I found him to be out of touch with reality. He explained that he consulted with the leaders of China and Russia, and he was more in touch with what was happening there than he was with what was happening in the US. Truly great strategists understand not only their opponents but also their own strengths and weaknesses. In our case, that means properly assessing the mood of the American public and what they think is most important. But his circle was made up entirely of elites, like Hillary Clinton. His friendship with her probably explains why he seemed bothered by the idea of a Trump presidency. Kissinger met with Trump and Jared Kushner, too, and I don't believe the president-elect was at all enamored with him either.

As the incoming NSA I also started speaking with counterparts around the world. Typically, the NSA is the most important adviser in governments around the world, whether they're led by presidents, prime ministers, or kings, since they have extensive knowledge and broad experience as well as a special relationship with the man, or woman, at the top.

I was also in contact with foreign ambassadors based in Washington. Some of the communications were merely protocol, but there were other ambassadors with whom we had urgent business, like the Israeli ambassador, Ron Dermer, and the Russian envoy, Sergei Kislyak. I'll discuss my conversations with both in some detail in the next chapter.

Normally, it's the State Department that handles relations with the diplomatic corps, but Rex Tillerson wasn't nominated as secretary of state until December, and it would take several months to get him through the Senate confirmation process. More importantly, I'd been speaking extensively with Trump about foreign policy for nearly a year and a half at that point. I knew his mind on international affairs and could genuinely speak for the president. It would take any secretary of state months to get up to speed on the direction of Trump's foreign policy and express his worldview. The unfortunate fact is that Tillerson never did.

The former CEO of Exxon had no government experience, but as a global industry leader, he knew heads of state all around the world, especially in the Middle East, which has been a major area of US concern for nearly a century precisely because of its energy reserves. Plus, since he'd run a huge company, the idea was that he could step right in and run a large organization like the State Department. But as often happens to those hired to run Foggy Bottom, he was captured by it. Rather than directing foreign service officers to serve the policies of the man Americans elected to make foreign policy, he represented the interests of the State Department and its career bureaucrats.

It wasn't surprising when Tillerson ended his tenure by stabbing Trump in the back. In all my years in uniform and then in Washington, I've seen many well-known figures tapped for cabinet posts more worried about their reputations and impressing their professional circles than they are serving the country. That was certainly the case with Tillerson.

I was involved in the discussions about nominating James Mattis for secretary of defense. I knew him personally, and with his credentials I certainly didn't have to vouch for him, but the president-elect did ask me about him and I said he was a professional who could get the job done. What I didn't realize was that Mattis had gotten involved in some strange business dealings after retiring from the Marine Corps. He joined the board of Theranos, the biotech company that claimed to have revolutionized blood testing—a scam that ripped off investors. Kissinger was also on the board. In 2023, Theranos's founder and CEO, Elizabeth Holmes, was sentenced to an eleven-year prison term for fraud. It was later reduced to nine years, a couple of months after she reported to prison. [29]

---

29 Integrity Line, "Elizabeth Holmes & Theranos: Lessons in Ethics and Compliance," *Integrity Line Blog*, August 1, 2023, https://www.integrityline.com/expertise/blog/elizabeth-holmes-theranos/.

Mattis also had an advisor named Sally Donnelly, who stewarded his confirmation process and assured Congress that Mattis would be the so-called adult in the room to keep Trump in line. It turned out that she had a financial arrangement with Amazon that led to speculation she'd leveraged her relationship with Mattis to get Amazon a $10 billion contract with the Pentagon.[30] The deal eventually fell through. And Mattis was a big disappointment. There were orders coming from the commander-in-chief that Mattis refused to implement, an astonishing turn for a man who knows as well as anyone that the chain of command is our military's central principle and civilian command of the military is a keystone of our form of government. He too took a cheap shot at the president on his way out of the administration.

Mike Pompeo was Trump's first CIA director, and I knew him as a congressman from his days on the House Intelligence Committee. Pompeo is a genuinely good guy and as a congressman was focused on Iran, which was helpful. He was at the top of his class at West Point and went to Harvard, but qualifications like that are less important than the ability to run large organizations. He didn't do a good job running the CIA or later the State Department. He was no Devin Nunes.

He should have done far more to expose the corruption inside the CIA, the State Department, and the intelligence community as a whole. He shirked his responsibility to Americans in both leadership positions by not helping to expose the criminal activities targeting the Trump administration.

Instead, it was left until very late in the Trump administration when acting Director of National Intelligence Richard Grenell and his deputy Kash Patel started declassifying documents and exposing the lies that drove Russiagate. Since so much of the unlawful activity came out of the CIA, starting with John Brennan, and the State

---

30 April Glaser, "How Amazon and Silicon Valley Seduced the Pentagon," *Mother Jones*, August 5, 2019, https://www.motherjones.com/politics/2019/08/how-amazon-and-silicon-valley-seduced-the-pentagon/.

Department, Pompeo had done a huge disservice to the president, and the country, by not helping to expose the criminal activities targeting the administration. To me this is unforgivable.

WHERE THE BODIES ARE BURIED

JFK is famously quoted as saying that he "wanted to splinter the C.I.A. in a thousand pieces and scatter it to the winds." My aim wasn't to break the CIA but to get it under control and ensure it served its mission, which is to collect and analyze intelligence for the executive in chief, who is elected by the public to implement foreign policy.

Looking back over the last several decades, it's hard to ignore what the intelligence community has gotten wrong—and it's no coincidence that during that same period, we've continued to lose wars and sacrifice the lives of courageous and patriotic young Americans. So we need to ask, why can't our spy chiefs get things right?

Just consider the serial failures of CIA directors in the last twenty years alone. George Tenet got Iraq's WMD program wrong.[31] John Brennan got Russiagate wrong—in fact, he lied about it, from the beginning to the present day.[32] James Woolsey made up that ridiculous story about me offering to kidnap Fethullah Gülen.[33] It's so crazy, that you're tempted to laugh, except it tells you a great deal about the character of the men who were chosen to lead our clandestine service.

Character is crucial, and the tragic fact for our country is that many of the people who have been named to important positions are just in it for themselves.

---

31 Scott Shane and Mark Mazzetti, "Ex-C.I.A. Chief, in Book, Assails Cheney on Iraq," *New York Times*, April 27, 2007, https://www.nytimes.com/2007/04/27/washington/27intel.html.

32 John H. Durham, Special Counsel, "Report on Matters Related to Intelligence Activities and Investigations Arising Out of the 2016 Presidential Campaigns," to Attorney General Merrick Garland, United States Department of Justice, May 12, 2023, https://www.justice.gov/storage/durhamreport.pdf.

33 Ken Dilanian, "Ex-CIA Director Spoke to Mueller about Flynn's Alleged Turkish Scheme," NBC News, October 27, 2017, https://www.nbcnews.com/politics/donald-trump/ex-cia-director-spoke-mueller-about-flynn-s-alleged-turkish-n815176.

And it's not just about bad individuals, it's also about the system itself. There are lots of programs, including very expensive programs, and billion-dollar programs, that don't serve our national interests. They're good for Beltway budgets, both the public sector and contractors and companies in the private sector, but they don't serve the American people, and I was named NSA by a president who promised accountability.

I knew going in about some of these programs and the budget allocations. And I knew who was making money from them, billions of dollars. Congress is supposed to control the purse strings; in particular, that's the job of the "gang of eight"—the Senate and House leadership as well as the heads of the intelligence committees from both parties in the House and Senate. But some of those lawmakers aren't up to it. Devin Nunes was an exception on the House Intelligence Committee, as chair and ranking member. More often than not, the intelligence community recruits lawmakers, so they take the side of the agencies, against the president and the electorate. I'd seen all that even before I was DIA director. That's what Trump aides and allies meant when they said, "Flynn knows where the bodies are buried."

I made it known that I was going to dig in and audit these programs to see what US taxpayers were getting for their money. If those programs weren't serving any purpose except to fill intelligence community budgets, then they were going to stop.

One of the first big briefings was with Vice President-elect Mike Pence in the transition headquarters at the General Services Administration Building in Washington used for presidential transitions. CIA leadership came in to brief us on certain programs, and I wanted details so that Pence had the information and that I had it for the president-elect. But they weren't prepared to brief us on the effectiveness of billion-dollar programs Instead it boiled down to, "Here's a program. It works great. And this is how much we spend on it." They told us that to answer any other of my questions, such as how effective this program or that program was, they were going to have to come back for a separate briefing, which turned out to be the same briefing but with more people. As if a bigger group made it more persuasive that the program was beneficial.

The fact is, they knew I was starting to dig in. And so, we're fighting a two-front battle—one with the intelligence community and another with the outgoing administration. The Obama team wasn't just hiding stuff from us, they were fighting us at every step.

As the incoming national security advisor, I was receiving constant reports about friction, resistance, hostility, and even subterfuge from the transition teams we put in each department, not just the national security and foreign policy shops like the Departments of Defense, Homeland Security, and State, but even from places like the Departments of Commerce and Agriculture. It seemed as though the outgoing personnel had been instructed not to cooperate, but rather to fight back against the new White House. And as we later learned, that's exactly what happened—and it started at the top, with the outgoing president, Barack Obama.

Many times I'd sworn the oath to protect and defend the country and Constitution from enemies, foreign and domestic. But I'd never really given much thought to domestic enemies. As a soldier and intelligence officer, I'd spent my career studying, facing, and fighting foreign adversaries. But as I began to see this new field of fight unfold before me, I came to recognize that the toughest battle in my life wasn't with an al-Qaeda leader, or on the plains of Eurasia against foreign troops from Russia or China. No, it would be the war that the US government had chosen to wage against me and Trump.

CHAPTER 9

ASSASSINATION BY NARRATIVE

SPYING ON THE TRANSITION TEAM

The clandestine surveillance operation targeting the Trump transition team began at the end of November, maybe earlier. But November 30 is when Barack Obama's UN ambassador, Samantha Power, first unmasked my name from a classified transcript of an intercept of me communicating with a foreign official.[34] As we later found out, there were at least forty Obama officials who unmasked my name from classified intercepts fifty-three times between that date and January 12, 2017—that's when the outgoing vice president, and later president, Joe Biden, did it.

The National Security Agency regularly collects on all sorts of foreign targets and sometimes picks up US citizens or permanent residents in those communications. Because our government is not supposed to be spying on us, the names of Americans are redacted—also called "minimizing" or "masking"—and identified only in the transcripts as "US Person," or some other generic qualifier. In my thirty-three years in the intelligence community operating at the highest levels of the government, I only had one unmasking request ever. It was to help discover financial transactions between a high-value terrorist target overseas we were hunting down and an American citizen. Even then, the American's name was only given to me (and I never leaked it).

---

34 Jeremy Herb and Marshall Cohen, "GOP Senators Release List of Obama Officials in Latest Effort to Undermine Russia Probe," CNN Politics, May 15, 2020, https://www.cnn.com/2020/05/13/politics/republican-list-obama-officials-unmask/index.html.

Sometimes analysts unmask an identity to better understand a particular national security issue. But it's done much less frequently by top-level officials who deal with big policy initiatives. And yet in my case, almost all the big names in the Obama administration were doing it. John Brennan, James Clapper, James Comey, Obama's Chief of Staff Denis McDonough, Treasury Secretary Jacob Lew, and several other Treasury officials, including the director of Treasury's intelligence agency, Office of Intelligence and Analysis, as well as several diplomats, like the ambassadors to Russia, Turkey, and Italy. They all unmasked my identity. It was one giant free-for-all.[35]

Samantha Power was at the top of the list, unmasking me seven times, a fraction of her personal surveillance campaign, which amounted to hundreds of unmaskings of US citizens between 2015 and 2016. According to former Congressman Trey Gowdy, Power is the "largest unmasker of U.S. persons in our history."

Why was the Obama team unmasking me? To leak my name and selectively edited portions of my conversations with foreign officials to the press. And leaking from those classified intercepts is a felony.[36]

There were constant leaks. I didn't know exactly what was going on at the time, but I had an idea something was vastly wrong. More and more damaging articles were coming out after President Trump appointed me as his incoming NSA. Immediately after I was appointed, I became the conduit between every world leader and President-elect Trump. Every day I'd set up five to ten foreign leader phone calls between him and presidents, kings, and premiers. I listened in on every single one of the calls, and each was transcribed

---

35 Memorandum for Director of National intelligence, from Paul M. Nakasone, National Security Agency, Follow-up Unmasking Request re Former National Security Advisor, May 4, 2020, pp. 3–5, https://www.hsgac.senate.gov/wp-content/uploads/imo/media/doc/2020-05-13%20ODNI%20to%20CEG%20RHJ%20(Unmasking).pdf. Note: Acting Director Richard Grenell, Office of the Director of National Intelligence, sent an unclassified copy of this memorandum to Senator Charles Grassley, Chairman, Committee on Finance, and Senator Ron Johnson, Chairman, Committee on Homeland Security, on May 13, 2020.

36 David Ignatius, "Why Did Obama Dawdle on Russia's Hacking?" *Washington Post*, January 12, 2017, https://www.washingtonpost.com/opinions/why-did-obama-dawdle-on-russias-hacking/2017/01/12/75f878a0-d90c-11e6-9a36-1d296534b31e_story.html.

by an interpreter when there was a language issue. The National Security Agency has every single phone call. Most were to simply congratulate Trump for winning. Some were to begin to set the stage for follow-up foreign policy discussions or visits. All should have been kept from the media unless the incoming Trump administration wanted to share any of the calls' contents with the media.

What I saw was that many pieces of these calls were being strategically leaked to damage Trump. The media wanted to show a chaotic Trump who didn't know how to deal with foreign leaders. I can tell you, having been on the majority of these calls, and then always following up with my national security foreign counterparts from each respective country, all were very positive; most said they hadn't spoken to Obama or anyone in his White House in months and many for much longer periods than that.

This is part of what I mean when I say that the transition from the Obama administration to the Trump administration was anything but normal. It was made exceedingly difficult by the fact that everything we did was immediately leaked to Obama allies in the media. I became even more suspicious about the Obama team's intentions in November and December because it appeared the media were asking questions about things going on with the transition team that they shouldn't have known about.

For example, we were making calls to select nations about the UN vote on Israel or the Obama administration's position on Russian sanctions and expulsions. These were issues we wanted to weigh in on but in no way meant to stop bad policy decisions, which these clearly were, but to let certain nations' representatives know what our policy positions were going to be as we were about to transition into the White House.

The outgoing administration made these major strategic decisions with only a few weeks remaining and never briefed our national security transition team on either of these critical actions. That would have been a sign of mutual respect, but the Obama administration showed none for the incoming Trump team. It was very clear to us from just these two examples that the Obama administration was purposely trying to damage our ability to work with these nations in the future or to conduct future foreign policy.

They spied on us through our conversations with foreign officials. They weren't interested in what our foreign counterparts were saying—it was us they were zeroed in on. It's called reverse targeting, and it's illegal. They arranged to have more reporting on foreign officials speaking to the Trump team or about it, then they'd leak it to the media. And my name was given to the press in what Devin Nunes called one of the biggest leaks in US history, which I'll go into shortly.

Eventually, Devin would go public with what he'd found as chairman of the House Permanent Select Committee on Intelligence (HPSCI). During a press conference on Capitol Hill in early spring 2017, he said, "I recently confirmed on numerous occasions, the U.S. intelligence community incidentally collected information about U.S. citizens in the Trump transition. Details about U.S. persons associated with the incoming administration, details with little or no apparent foreign intelligence value were widely disseminated in intelligence community reporting. I have confirmed that additional names of Trump transition team members were unmasked."[37]

In other words, the outgoing Obama administration was unmasking not just me but also other Trump transition officials. It was a full-on surveillance campaign targeting Obama's political opponents.

At the same time that there was a clandestine surveillance campaign targeting us, there was also a public campaign against the Trump team, and me in particular. There were stories about me in the media claiming I was something of a dictator and wouldn't allow disagreements with my intelligence assessments at DIA. Nothing could have been further from the truth. As an intelligence officer in a war zone, and then as an intelligence chief, I urged my team to think outside the box and challenge the received wisdom. The mission is

37 "Chairman Nunes Comments on Incidental Collection of Trump Associates," Permanent Select Committee on Intelligence, press release, March 22, 2017, https://intelligence.house.gov/news/documentsingle.aspx?DocumentID=774.

not about winning internal arguments but getting to the truth to serve Americans, on the battlefield or in the homeland.

The press reported that, in my view, America was in a world war against Islamist militants allied with powerful state actors. They were right on that front—I did and I believe it still. I didn't take it as a smear.

These stories were used by progressive advocacy groups that had allied with the Obama White House to push through the disastrous Iran nuclear deal. These groups complained about my views on Islamic extremism and Iran and demanded Trump withdraw my appointment. But the president-elect was as eager as I was to undo the Iran deal, and I was running point on that. I'd served in two Middle Eastern theaters of combat and saw how the Iranians had murdered our troops in Iraq especially, as well as Afghanistan. Legalizing a terror state's nuclear weapons program, as the Iran deal did, was a disaster for long-term US government interests and security abroad and at home.

US allies who were especially worried about the Iran deal included not just Israel, maybe the prospective number one target for an Iranian nuke, but also our Arab allies in the Gulf, like the United Arab Emirates (UAE).

In the middle of December, Jared Kushner, Steve Bannon, and I met with the crown prince of the UAE, Mohammed bin Zayed Al Nahyan, often referred to as MBZ. He is a dramatic and impressive figure, almost like out of a movie. He's very sophisticated, highly intelligent, and sharp. MBZ told us that he wanted a much stronger relationship with the US and that his relationship personally with Obama was nonexistent. And he and key members of his team told us they could not stand Susan Rice—most people, especially all my foreign counterparts I interacted with said similar things about her.

There was a lot to set right. ISIS was a significant problem, Afghanistan was still raging, Iraq was on the rocks, and the US was operating in Syria too. We needed eyes and ears in the region we could trust, and the UAE had been a traditional US partner in the

Middle East—until Obama overturned the order of the region to build a potential partnership with Iran, the world's leading state sponsor of terror. We were turning that around. MBZ and his team trusted me because of my background. We connected. Many of them were either intelligence or special operation types.

As Nunes's intelligence committee later discovered, this was another meeting that the Obama team had used to spy on us—and it was Susan Rice herself who unmasked me. She said she wanted to know why MBZ had come to the United States without notifying the Obama White House.[38] That's ridiculous—and it doesn't explain why she unmasked the identities of Trump transition officials.

In fact, she and dozens of other Obama officials unmasked me on account of that meeting.[39] And it's not hard to see why—spying on our meetings with Arab leaders would tell them how our policies would affect Obama's initiatives, especially the Iran deal. The fact that officials from the Treasury Department were spying on that meeting says they wanted to know if Trump was planning to restore the sanctions on Iran that Obama undid to clinch the nuclear deal with Iran. Members of the Obama administration were bordering on, if not committing, treason.

38 Manu Raju, "Exclusive: Rice Told House Investigators Why She Unmasked Senior Trump Officials, CNN, September 13, 2017,https://www.cnn.com/2017/09/13/politics/susan-rice-house-investigators-unmasked-trump-officials/index.html

39 Memorandum for Director of National Intelligence, from Paul M. Nakasone, National Security Agency, Follow-up Unmasking Request re Former National Security Advisor, May 4, 2020, pp. 3–5, https://www.hsgac.senate.gov/wp-content/uploads/imo/media/doc/2020-05-13%20ODNI%20to%20CEG%20RHJ%20(Unmasking).pdf. Note: Acting Director Richard Grenell, Office of the Director of National Intelligence, sent an unclassified copy of this memorandum to Senator Charles Grassley, Chairman, Committee on Finance, and Senator Ron Johnson, Chairman, Committee on Homeland Security, on May 13, 2020.

DESTABILIZING THE TRANSITION—
AND THE COUNTRY

There was so much that we had to set in order. And the Obama team was hell-bent on stopping us, and they got plenty of help from the media, which just fired barrage after barrage of lies at us.

Maybe I shouldn't have been surprised, but even after being forced out of the Obama administration for telling the truth, I still couldn't believe that they could, or would, twist reality to fit their political narrative no matter how much it hurt the country.

It was hard sometimes to keep count of all the snares the outgoing administration set for us. But I remember one I couldn't ignore. In the second week of December, *The Washington Post* published an article claiming that "the CIA has concluded in a secret assessment that Russia intervened in the 2016 election to help Donald Trump win the presidency, rather than just to undermine confidence in the U.S. electoral system."[40]

Further, according to the report, Obama told CIA Director John Brennan to conduct a full review of all intelligence relating to Russia and the 2016 elections and have it ready by the time he left office on January 20.

This was shocking for a number of reasons. First, assuming the story came from the CIA, that "secret" assessment was classified. Someone high up in the agency was leaking classified information. And more significantly, it was weaponized to target the president-elect and undermine the new administration. I knew from experience there was no way the intelligence community could complete a genuine assessment in a month and a half, especially not during the Christmas season when even the federal government grinds to a halt. And they weren't going to—as the article showed, they'd already

---

40   Adam Entous, Ellen Nakashima, and Greg Miller, "Secret CIA Assessment Says Russia Was Trying to Help Trump Win White House," *Washington Post*, December 9, 2016, https://www.washingtonpost.com/world/national-security/obama-orders-review-of-russian-hacking-during-presidential-campaign/2016/12/09/31d6b300-be2a-11e6-94ac-3d324840106c_story.html.

come to their phony conclusion: Putin helped Trump win the White House. This was a monumental hit job, a political assassination by narrative of President-elect Trump, unlike anything we'd ever seen before in US history.

Maybe it's good to take a step back after all this time and try to comprehend what happened with this leak. The Clinton campaign had tried to defeat Trump with a dirty trick, smearing him, me, and his aides as Russian agents. But now the presidential race was over; Trump won. It was time for the country to move on, solve its problems, and resolve its differences through normal political processes on Capitol Hill and in the White House.

But that's not how Obama wanted it. Instead, under his orders, the CIA gave its official stamp of approval to an insane and divisive conspiracy theory. Obama wanted to delegitimize the new White House—and also the voters who put Trump there. If the new president was a foreign agent, then his supporters were at best dupes, if not willing accomplices of a Russian plot to infiltrate the US government. In other words, Obama was calling at least half the country disloyal or traitorous. He destabilized not just the new administration but the country as a whole by setting us against each other. He not only perverted the peaceful transfer of power, he also put us on course for domestic conflict.

Of course, if you see the Obama administration in its full context, splitting the country into good guys and bad ones was normal for the outgoing president. Whenever it came time to market another of his harmful domestic or foreign policies, he rolled out his favorite slogan to attack his opponents—"That's not who we are as Americans," he said time and again. All he meant was that he had the last say over who was really American: anyone who opposed him. Since I crossed his political narrative and said that al-Qaeda wasn't finished and that Sunni extremists were gathering strength, I guess that made me, a combat veteran with thirty-three years in uniform, un-American in his eyes.

I know one thing for sure: There were lots of reasons the outgoing president and his team might have had for targeting me. I did know where the bodies were buried, still do; I was intent on dismantling the Deep State infrastructure; and I was dead set against the Iran deal and determined to do anything to serve President Trump to withdraw from it. But the fact that I challenged Obama's narrative in public was something he'd never forget.

OBAMA BETRAYING ALLIES

The president-elect was an outsider who was bringing some outsiders to fix Washington. The one drawback with political outsiders is that no one on the transition team really knew foreign officials. Nor were they known in foreign capitals by our allies and other powers. But I did know foreign ambassadors, foreign ministers, and intelligence officials around the world. I knew presidents and kings, and they knew me. Some I'd served alongside abroad, and others I'd dealt with in some professional capacity, so it was my role on the transition team to speak with the world.

That's what the transition team is supposed to be doing: setting the table for the incoming administration so the new president can dig in right away. But the Obama administration was sucking the wind out of us with their last-minute foreign policy projects.

A normal president during the transition process would continue to manage the country and stay ready for any national security emergency. After all, it's a vulnerable period, with one administration wrapping things up and another preparing to come to power. And you don't know if one of our adversaries might seize the opportunity to attack us. But aside from that, the outgoing president should do little to change the course of events, never mind get in its last blows at the opposition party as it comes to power. With the election, the nation has spoken. That's how our constitutional republic should work, and that precedent has been long established. And Obama broke it.

As stated above, Obama wanted one last parting shot at Israel, and he took it with UN Security Council 2334, holding that Israel was occupying the territories it had taken in the June 1967 war. According to UNSCR 2334, Israel was in "flagrant violation" of international law.[41] Under the terms of the resolution, even the Western Wall of the Temple Mount, the holiest site in Judaism, was an illegal Israeli settlement.

This was the position held by the Arab rejectionist camp—that the Israelis were "occupying" the ancient capital of Israel. To believe this, you have to be not only a pro-Palestinian ideologue but also entirely ignorant of Judeo-Christian history. The Temple is a real place that was first built by King David's son Solomon. It appears all throughout the Old and New Testaments. That American elites are so arrogant to ignore the Bible, the foundation of American civilization, as well as the historical and archeological record tells you a lot about where we are right now as a country.

Obama hated Israel, according to Susan Rice. She pretty much told me that when we were together in her office during one of our transition interactions. Her oozing arrogance over Israel's positions regarding Iran and Iranian surrogates like Hezbollah and Hamas was thick enough to make me feel ill.

The United Nations resolution represented a huge betrayal by the United States. The Israelis were very upset but knew that the incoming administration was going to have their back. I had many discussions with the Israeli ambassador to the US at the time, Ron Dermer. Ron is a real professional and brilliant strategic thinker. He and I knew each other from before, and in my meetings with him and Israeli intelligence officials, I told them I was confident that we'd soon get past what the Obama team had in the works, regardless of how much pain it was designed to cause our Middle East ally.

In the meantime, I set to work. The outgoing administration had strong-armed Egypt into introducing the resolution, but President-

---

41 Benjamin Weinthal, "Critics Charge Biden with Abandoning Israel, Hostages amid Growing Tensions with Jewish State," Fox News, March 27, 2024, https://www.foxnews.com/world/critics-charge-biden-abandoning-israel-hostages-growing-tensions-jewish-state.

elect Trump convinced Egyptian President Abdel Fattah El-Sisi to withdraw the proposal. But we knew the Obama team would get someone else to sponsor it.

So, I got on the phone and spoke with a number of foreign officials. I knew that at least five countries had to abstain to block the resolution, so I didn't think my calls would affect the final vote. I compared the exercise to a battle drill, to see how quickly I could get foreign officials on the phone.

The final vote was scheduled for December 23, and that day I spoke with the Russian ambassador to Washington, Sergei Kislyak. I'd developed a relationship with Ambassador Kislyak previously, as I had with many foreign officials in Washington over the years. He's a decent man, a grandfatherly-looking Russian who perhaps smokes too many cigars and sniffs a little bit too much whiskey.

We talked about the vote that day, and he said for "historical reasons" Moscow couldn't vote against the resolution. The Middle East had been a Cold War battlefield, and for nearly fifty years the Russians contested American power in the region. Since they still supported and armed Syria and other enemies of our ally Israel, the Russians had no choice but to support the resolution.

I told him I understood. He said they might help delay the vote to give us time, and I was grateful, even though I knew there was little chance we'd prevent the resolution from going through.

And that day the UN passed Security Council Resolution 2334 by a vote of 14–0, with Samantha Power casting the American vote to abstain. Historically the US has defended Israel at the UN by vetoing disgustingly anti-Israel resolutions, but not this time. Obama's UN ambassador sided with the jackals. And naturally, as I found out later, Samantha Power had spied on my December 23 conversation with Kislyak.

KISLYAK CALLING

As December wound down and the new year approached, Lori and I wanted to take a vacation because with my work in the White House, this was probably going to be our last chance to get away for a while. There was no doubt I was going to be working all day and night seven days a week. We decided on the Dominican Republic because we had been there before and really enjoyed it. We were planning on a short week, and it ended up even shorter because of everything happening back in Washington.

I hadn't seen all the news reports coming in, but I was on the phone with my deputies and others back in Washington. And the big news was that the Obama administration had taken some actions against the Russians, supposedly to punish them for interfering in the election. The transition team found out about it in the media like the rest of the world.

On December 29, Obama expelled thirty-five Russian diplomats that his administration assessed were intelligence agents. He also closed two diplomatic facilities, one in New York and another in Maryland,[42] and sanctioned officials from Russian military intelligence, including the head of the GRU, Igor Korobov, who'd succeeded Igor Sergun.

My immediate thought was that between the Israel vote at the UN and now the expulsions, the Obama administration was doing all it could to create chaos for us.

My next thought was that Obama was playing with fire. Here he was advancing a political narrative designed to advance Democratic Party interests in the domestic arena, and potentially provoking a very powerful Russian government. It was bad enough that the Clinton campaign had dragged Russia and Putin personally into her dirty

---

42 Lauren Gambino, Sabrina Siddiqui, and Shaun Walker, "Obama Expels 35 Russian Diplomats in Retaliation for US Election Hacking," *The Guardian*, December 30, 2016, https://www.theguardian.com/us-news/2016/dec/29/barack-obama-sanctions-russia-election-hack.

tricks operation. Now the outgoing president was punching Putin in the nose to make the Democrats' conspiracy theory look real.

That same day, I spoke with Ambassador Kislyak on the phone. He had a few items to discuss about the Middle East, but obviously his big concern was the actions Obama had taken. The phone reception down in the Dominican Republic made it even harder for me to understand his thick Russian accent.

I told him that I understood Moscow would have to respond. I asked him to make it reciprocal. I know you're going to have to do something, but I said, "don't go any further than you have to. Because I don't want us to get into something that has to escalate, on a tit-for-tat."

I'm being honest with him because it wasn't our call. It was Obama. I said, "Do not allow this administration to box us in."

He knew exactly what I meant. "It's very specifically and transparently, openly," he said, referring to Obama's efforts to force his successor's hand with Russia. Kislyak said that I had to "appreciate the sentiments that are raging now in Moscow."

"I do appreciate it," I said. "But I really don't want us to get into a situation where we do this and then you do something bigger, and then everybody's going back and forth, and everybody's got to be the tough guy." I continued: "We need cool heads to prevail, and we need to be very steady about what we're going to do because we have absolutely a common threat in the Middle East right now." I was referring to Islamic extremism.

Kislyak said he was going "to try to get the people in Moscow to understand it," and we talked about the Middle East a little more and then said our farewells.

On December 30, Russian President Vladimir Putin announced: "Although we have the right to retaliate, we will not resort to irresponsible 'kitchen' diplomacy but will plan our further steps to restore Russian-U.S. relations based on the policies of the Trump Administration."

By New Year's Eve, Lori and I were back in Washington, DC, and I got another call from Ambassador Kislyak. He said he had a small message to pass to me from Moscow, that our conversation from the twentieth-ninth was taken into account, and my proposal to act with cool heads influenced Moscow's decision to not escalate. I told him I appreciated his feedback, and after a brief back-and-forth on the Middle East, we concluded our call.

I have to admit that I felt pretty good about myself right then. I'd asked for our Russian counterparts to understand the situation, and they did. I mean, I wasn't patting myself on the back for averting World War III, but it was a useful diplomatic win that prevented a bad situation not of our own making from getting worse, maybe much worse.

Of course, I knew that call and all my calls with Kislyak were being monitored by US agencies and probably others. [43] The Russian ambassador's communications are going to be intercepted, and speaking with him meant I was also picked up. And the NSA in any US presidential administration is going to be a surveillance target for almost every intelligence service in the world. What I didn't know at the time, what I could not have possibly imagined, is that our own intelligence agencies would use that December 29 call to try to destroy me.

BRENNAN'S TREACHERY

On January 6, the declassified version of Brennan's intelligence community assessment (ICA) was released.[44] It was laughable. You don't have to be a trained intelligence professional to know that it was a childish and amateurish piece of work.

---

43   Kristina Wong, "Documents: Obama Knew Details of Michael Flynn's Call with Russian Ambassador," Breitbart, May 8, 2017, https://www.breitbart.com/politics/2020/05/08/michael-flynn-documents-obama-knew-details-call-russian-ambassador/.

44   Director of National Intelligence, *Background to "Assessing Russian Activities and Intentions in Recent US Elections": The Analytic Process and Cyber Incident Attribution,"* ICA 2017-01D, January 6, 2017, https://www.dni.gov/files/documents/ICA_2017_01.pdf.

First of all, it was only four agencies that contributed to the assessment. The US intelligence community comprises seventeen agencies, and the ICA didn't include, among others, the State Department or my former agency, the DIA, both of which have good capabilities on Russia. Remember, I was the first to visit Russian military intelligence headquarters, while the CIA under Obama didn't see Russia as a priority. And the National Security Agency, which is responsible for collecting electronic communications, supported the key assessment, that Putin wanted to help Trump win, only with moderate confidence—which probably meant there was no signals intelligence corroborating the ICA's key finding.

Some of the assertions backing that finding are just plain ridiculous, like this one: "Beginning in June, Putin's public comments about the U.S. presidential race avoided directly praising President-elect Trump, probably because Kremlin officials thought that any praise from Putin personally would backfire in the United States." Okay, so part of the evidence that Putin supported Trump is that he avoided praising Trump.

It was a total embarrassment for the intelligence community as a whole—except we now know it wasn't the IC that produced it. No, it was just a bunch of Brennan acolytes. He kept his team small to keep everyone else out, according to one former intelligence official who spoke with a reporter.

Brennan didn't want anyone looking at process, methodology, and tradecraft. "The flawed methodology and tradecraft obscured reporting that pointed in the opposite direction of the conclusion Brennan sought," according to the US official who'd seen the data. In fact, it suggested that the Russians preferred Clinton.

"The Russians assumed she would win," the former official said. "They had experience with her and knew how to manage her.[45] The ICA also obscured reporting that the Russians saw lots of problems

---

45   Jack Cashill, "Why the CIA Is Hiding the 'Putin Loves Hillary' Report," World NetDaily, February 22, 2024, https://www.wnd.com/2024/02/cia-hiding-putin-loves-hillary-report/.

in a potential Trump presidency, given his personality and the like-lihood that he'd take a harder line approach with them." Brennan, according to the official, "wanted to avoid scrutiny because he was purposefully manipulating intelligence to go one way to support this illusion that Trump had colluded with Russia. That's fraud."[46]

And Brennan based the assessment on the phony Trump-Russia dossier that was funded by the Clinton campaign. Brennan would eventually tell Congress that the dossier was not used in the ICA, but it was.[47]

According to the intelligence official, "A summary of the dossier was attached to the ICA in a two-page document called Annex A. The ICA's principal finding is that Russia's influence campaign aspired to help Trump, but the footnote to support that key judgment refers to Annex A, which is the dossier."

The ICA was poison, and Obama knew it when he asked Brennan to produce it because Brennan had told him months before. In August, as documents later declassified by Trump's director of national intelligence, John Ratcliffe, showed, and Special Counsel John Durham's report demonstrated, Brennan even briefed Obama on the dossier and told him that the Clinton campaign was running a dirty tricks operation to smear Trump as a Russian agent. But Brennan pressed on anyway.

As he bragged to Devin's committee a few months after I left the White House, Brennan said he "was aware of intelligence and information about contacts between Russian officials and U.S. persons."

Brennan said that he "wanted to make sure that every information and bit of intelligence that we had was shared with the Bureau so that they could take it." But, of course, there was no evidence tying Russian officials to the Trump team. The CIA director wanted credit

46   Matt Taibbi, Michael Shellenberger, and Alex Gutentag, "CIA 'Cooked the Intelligence' to Hide That Russia Favored Clinton, Not Trump, in 2016, Sources Say," Public News, February 15, 2024, https://public.substack.com/p/cia-cooked-the-intelligence-to-hide.

47   Brooke Singman, "Newly Declassified Intel Document Noted Steele Dossier Claims Had 'Limited Corroboration,'" Fox News, June 11, 2020, https://www.foxnews.com/politics/ica-steele-dossier-claims.

for his role interfering in the 2016 election and then undermining an American president. He was coming after me too. I threatened not only his standing but also the legacy he'd built at the CIA in his own pompous and destructive image.

As one former senior intelligence official told a reporter, "Flynn was the biggest threat to the CIA the agency had seen in years." *Fixing Intel* put the CIA on notice. According to that official, it "worried the Agency a great deal.... The model that 'Fixing Intel' called for was, if not diametrically opposed to the interests of the CIA, at least represented a significantly different approach." And that's why, according to former Senate staffer and longtime intelligence expert Angelo Codevilla, I had to be eliminated. "Not just because of Trump, but because of Flynn himself," the late Codevilla told a journalist. Flynn, he said, "was an existential threat to the CIA."[48]

48 Angelo Codevilla, "Abolish FISA, Reform FBI, & Break Up CIA," *The American Mind*, February 12, 2020, https://americanmind.org/memo/abolish-the-cia/.

CHAPTER 10

GET FLYNN

THE SETUP

During Barack Obama's January 5 meeting in the White House, his deputies James Comey, Susan Rice, Joe Biden, Jim Clapper, John Brennan, and others gathered to discuss how to take me down in an operation designed to collapse the incoming president, destabilize our government, and divide America. The operation began for real exactly one week later. On January 12, *The Washington Post* published a column stating:

> *According to a senior U.S. government official, Flynn phoned Russian Ambassador Sergey Kislyak several times on Dec. 29th, the day the Obama administration announced the expulsion of 35 Russian officials as well as other measures in retaliation for the hacking. What did Flynn say, and did it undercut the U.S. sanctions? The Logan Act (though never enforced) bars U.S. citizens from correspondence intending to influence a foreign government about "disputes" with the United States.* [49]

With this, that US government official broke the law by leaking information from a classified foreign intelligence intercept. The author of the article was David Ignatius, notorious in Washington, DC, circles as a messenger for intelligence agencies, US and foreign. When intelligence officers here or abroad are looking to send a signal

---

[49]   David Ignatius, "Opinion: Why Did Obama Dawdle on Russia's Hacking?" *Washington Post*, January 12, 2017, https://www.washingtonpost.com/opinions/why-did-obama-dawdle-on-russias-hacking/2017/01/12/75f878a0-d90c-11e6-9a36-1d296534b31e_story.html.

147

that reverberates throughout the US government, an Ignatius column is sure to get widespread attention and leave his Beltway audience piecing together the puzzle. In this way, he's absolutely a part of intelligence community operations—he's part of the IC's communications infrastructure.

But with the operation targeting me, his role was much more active, as if he were a genuine spy. At the same time he used his column to prosecute an IC campaign against me by leaking my conversation with Kislyak, he was in fact a close friend of my incoming deputy, KT MacFarland.

I liked KT. I thought she was smart and very pro-Trump. She had served on the NSC staff previously under Henry Kissinger in the Richard Nixon administration and served at the Pentagon during the Ronald Reagan administration. She was well-connected in Washington circles and often referred to as a Kissinger protégé. Her time with Fox News was a benefit because it allowed her to have a good media network. I thought she could help, and I asked Trump to hire her as my deputy. We went to work to put together the staff, and we had a good and honest relationship at first.

She told me she and Ignatius were good friends. In her own book, she described a January 10 event at the US Institute of Peace where Susan Rice and I both spoke. At the end of the dinner, a journalist at her table offered to share a cab and drop her at her home. KT didn't name him in her book, but the journalist was Ignatius, and it was on a phone call during this cab ride that James Clapper told Ignatius to "take the kill shot" on me. Two days later, Ignatius's article came out.

Of course, I only learned all about this when I read it much later. KT never said anything to me about it. It's understandable if she was embarrassed by what happened and her connection to the media operative who was instructed to bring me down, but she should have told me, not just for my sake but also for the sake of the administration and the country. That article helped revive the Russia lie that would have otherwise died. As Devin Nunes has said, "The Russia story was reenergized with the Flynn leak."[50] And it led to my exit from the White House.

I don't blame KT. But the fact is that the waters of the swamp run so deep that there's plenty of room for those from supposedly opposing sides to meet.

What a lot of people don't know is that Ignatius was the second choice for that leak. It was first offered to his *Post* colleague Adam Entous. At the time, according to Entous, "his sources start whispering…that there were all these mysterious communications between Michael Flynn" and Kislyak. Entous said he didn't know what to make of it. At the *Post*, he said, "There are divisions about this. Why is it news that Michael Flynn is talking to the Russian ambassador? He should be talking to the Russian ambassador. He should be talking to him about saving the children of Aleppo, for example. There's no reason why he shouldn't be having that conversation."

Entous played a key role in the get Flynn operation, but he was right on that one count: There was nothing "mysterious" about me communicating with Kislyak.[51] It was my job.

Entous was one of the real drivers of Russiagate. He was fed countless leaks of classified information from past and serving intelligence officials to advance the Trump-Russia lie. It's clear he's plugged into the CIA and trusted to take out their laundry—for instance, he wrote the December 9 article about the CIA's "secret" assessment that Putin helped Trump win the 2016 election.

On January 5, the day of Obama's big White House meeting with Biden, Rice, Comey, and others, Entous published an article claiming that US intelligence agencies "intercepted communications in the

---

50 Rep. Nunes unpacks the FBI and Mainstream Media's corrupt efforts to set up Lt. Gen. Michael Flynn www.youtube.com/watch?v=1U5OrT0skY0.

51 Adam Entous and Greg Miller, "U.S. Intercepts Capture Senior Russian Officials Celebrating Trump Win," *Washington Post*, January 5, 2017, https://www.washingtonpost.com/world/national-security/us-intercepts-capture-senior-russian-officials-celebrating-trump-win/2017/01/05/d7099406-d355-11e6-9cb0-54ab630851e8_story.html.

aftermath of the election in which Russian officials congratulated themselves on the outcome."[52]

The point of the article was to keep sustaining the conspiracy theory that Russia helped Trump win. In fact, what the article really signaled was that Entous's sources, US officials, had leaked what looks like another foreign intelligence intercept—another felony. The leak campaign was, in fact, a crime spree of historic proportions.[53]

But there's something else that needs to be investigated: According to my sources in the media, Entous was also close to Joe Biden's staff, in particular the then-vice president's national security advisor, Colin Kahl, who held the number three position in the Pentagon in the early days of the Biden presidency. And it's sure notable that in Ignatius's article he mentioned the Logan Act, an obscure statute that Biden first raised in Obama's January 5 meeting in the Oval Office. So the question stuck in my mind is: Did Biden, the man who was later elected to be president, or his aides play a role in framing me by illegally leaking a foreign intelligence intercept?

PENCE FOLDS

It's true that the incoming White House was largely unfamiliar with the ways of Washington. Spokesmen spent so much time batting down the Ignatius article and other stories when it would have been better to not say anything. It was obvious the outgoing administration and the press were trying to hang Russia around our necks like an albatross. And anything we said was just going to be twisted around until it served their purposes, not ours. You can chalk some of it up to

---

52 Entous and Miller, "U.S. Intercepts Capture Senior Russian Officials Celebrating Trump Win."

53 Techno Fog (@Techno_Fog), "The INITIAL Flynn/Kislyak leak was not to David Ignatius—it was to WaPo reporter Adam Entous," Twitter (now X), May 10, 2020, https://x.com/Techno_Fog/status/1259582006784032770?ref_src=twsrc%5Etf-w%7Ctwcamp%5Etweetembed%7Ctwterm%5E1259582006784032770%7Ctw gr%5E8ad436e46c208ddd8713f8b7bca53ca704c0b4a2%7Ctwcon%5Es1_&ref_url=https%3A%2F%2Fwww.thegatewaypundit.com%2F2020%2F05%2Fdevelen-tous-leak-came-directly-sources-saw-transcript-described-entous%2F.

inexperience on our part, but there was another factor as well. Obama had stirred the country into a frenzy, just as he'd intended.

Within only a little more than two weeks, there were the expulsions of Russian personnel, Brennan's intelligence community assessment, the publication of the Steele dossier, the constant stream of leaks all related to Russia, and then the Ignatius article. None of this was really about Russia of course—the purpose was to undermine the new Trump administration. And the effect was to drive the country to the brink of madness.

None of this was normal for America. I've said that the transition period was like war for the incoming administration. But it was more too. It was as if the whole country was experiencing the dread and panic of a war America was destined to pay a heavy price for losing. And for good reason, so much propaganda had been pumped into our public space. It was as if our media had been taken over by a hostile power determined to demoralize us.

I've studied information warfare for much of my career—as a military intelligence officer and then as an intelligence chief. I know what it looks like, how it works, how to identify the operation's targets, who's pushing it, and what its ultimate goals are, so I understood we were in the middle of an information warfare campaign. After all I'd been through with Obama, maybe it shouldn't have surprised me—he'd told Trump not to hire me. But it was hard to comprehend at the time that we were in the middle of an existential campaign of information warfare waged against the entire country by our own agencies in partnership with the media.

The Ignatius article made clear that the first goal was to get rid of me by getting someone inside the Trump team to turn against me. Looking at it now, it's no surprise that it was Vice President-elect Mike Pence.

On January 15, Pence appeared on one of the Sunday morning news-talk shows, *Face the Nation*. He was asked about the Ignatius story and said that I had not discussed the sanctions with the Russian ambassador. "I can confirm, having spoken to him about it," said

Pence, referring to me, that I "did not discuss anything having to do with the United States' decision to expel diplomats or impose censure against Russia."[54]

Pence might have replied that he didn't want to discuss it. He could have said that the Russia issue touched on a matter of great importance to the administration, a national security affair he wasn't at liberty to discuss at that time. Or he might have pointed out that the Ignatius story was based on a leak of classified information and the Trump team was determined to get to the bottom of it and hold accountable the US official who broke the law.

Or he could have just said something like, it's five days before the inauguration, and I'm here to talk about the Trump administration's big plans for America. Pence might have used any of the boilerplate statements made on those shows every week to brush off questions politicians and bureaucrats don't want to answer and basically say, hey, it isn't any of your business. Whatever the NSA and I discussed about our policies or world leaders was no one's business but our own. We had a country to run—to fix really. A pushback like that would have ended this sorry chapter right there.

The reality is that when he and I spoke on the phone the night before he went on the air, we never discussed sanctions at all. It never came up because the Russian ambassador and I never discussed them. There was a lot else going on in the world, and I was preparing to lead the national security component of the new White House. The phony sanctions that Obama imposed to box us in and underscore the lie that Putin helped Trump win was not the most important thing on my mind.

But the fact is that if I had discussed sanctions it would have been a legitimate subject of conversation for the incoming NSA to have with the Russian envoy. I didn't want the president to start his first term with the threat of war looming over us. That could have

---

54 Mike Pence, Manchin, Newt Gingrich, *Face the Nation* transcript, CBS News, January 15, 2017, https://www.cbsnews.com/news/face-the-nation-transcript-january-15-2017-pence-manchin-gingrich/.

happened had the Russians decided to escalate it. All I asked them to do was not escalate.

But Pence's response to the news show host was weak. The question, like the Ignatius story, was made to put the administration on the defensive, and Pence folded. Yes, it was a hectic period for the administration and it's possible Pence just fell into a trap set for him by the FBI and the media. The other possibility is that he intended to drive a wedge between me and the president. I have always believed it was the latter.

I never felt at ease with Pence. His reaction to the *Access Hollywood* tape told me something about the man I couldn't forget. If he was willing to resign from the campaign because of a fake scandal that was used as an October surprise against Trump, how could the president count on him in the middle of a real crisis with American lives on the line? And if he was waiting for his establishment allies to push him into the top spot if Trump left the ticket, how could the president be sure of his number two's loyalty?

Pence again showed his character, or lack of it, in the coming days.

FBI AMBUSHES THE WHITE HOUSE

Pence and Reince Priebus were establishment insiders who showed their true colors when the *Access Hollywood* video was leaked as an October surprise. Now that Trump was president, their next move was to fill his administration with people to block the commander-in-chief's agenda. In other words, we were facing opponents inside as well as outside the administration.

A little more than a week after the inauguration, Comey told his deputy McCabe to send agents to interview me. McCabe called and said he wanted to send some people over to ask about my conversations with Kislyak. I looked at my schedule; I was sitting in the office doing some reading. I told the secretary out front, "Hey, a couple of guys from the FBI are going to come over." Then I told McCabe, "Of course, no problem"—and added, "You know what I said because you guys were probably listening."

In fact, we'd had the FBI come speak to the new White House team just the day before. I brought them over to talk to the staff about handling classified information and the threat of foreign espionage targeting anyone working in the White House. From experience and common sense, I knew that the staff was going to be approached by foreign agencies. The staff in this White House was green and knew little, if anything, about the world of espionage and counterintelligence. I knew that hostile countries would do anything—deceive them, coerce them—to get them to spy against their own country. It's only in retrospect that we can see the chief espionage threat against the Trump White House was not foreign agencies, but our own.

Comey later bragged in front of a New York audience that sending over FBI agents to ambush the new national security advisor was something he "probably wouldn't have done or maybe gotten away with in a more organized…administration." The audience laughed loudly, which says all you need to know about the kind of deranged audiences that Comey attracts. With other administrations, he said, "if the FBI wanted to send agents into the White House itself to interview a senior official, you would work through the White House Counsel and there'd be discussions and approvals and it would be there. And I thought, it's early enough, let's just send a couple of guys over." The crowd laughed again.[55]

But there's nothing funny about what he did. He knew he was undermining the duly elected president of the United States and his staff and admitted he had violated protocol. And he was proud of it.

That was evil. The fact that Comey thought he could "get away with it" epitomizes the utter arrogance and disdain that the former director of the FBI had for the rule of law and the absence of any

---

55 Nicolle Wallace interview of James Comey, "New James Comey Revelations on Flynn, Trump Legal Jeopardy, Blackmail Concerns," *Deadline: White House*, MSNBC, December 10, 2018, viewed on YouTube, https://www.youtube.com/watch?v=NxNhj-FrjXqI, timestamp: 0:00-:30.

moral or ethical direction in his own life. He was proud of his effort to undermine the newly elected president by going after me. They could then focus their government subversives planted in critical positions around the government to get rid of Trump. Comey is the perfect illustration of the deep corruption within the culture of the FBI. This is the stuff that third world nations are known for.

What I didn't know at the time, and what wasn't revealed until FBI documents from the phony Crossfire Hurricane investigation were declassified in spring 2020, was that Comey and his team prepared in advance to set me up. In a meeting with Comey and McCabe, former head of counterintelligence Bill Priestap asked if the "goal" of the FBI's leadership was to get me "to lie, so we can prosecute him or get him fired."[56] Or, according to Priestap's notes, did they want me to admit to violating the Logan Act?

When I saw these notes much later, I was shocked. As the former head of an intelligence agency and at one time the president's national security advisor, I could barely believe the FBI was this corrupt. Priestap was the head of all the FBI's counterintelligence operations, domestically and globally. As the official responsible for rooting out the foreign spies who endanger our peace and prosperity this is one of the most important positions in the entire US government. It's bad enough Priestap was coordinating an espionage operation devised to take out the NSA and undermine the president. But what does it say about the FBI's record as a whole?

If they were so corrupt as to plot against the NSA, what else had they done in the past to disrupt the normal functioning of our constitutional republic? Were there other Americans they put in jail just because the FBI held a grudge against them? Moreover, if they were focused on getting Americans, who was watching out for real espionage operations run by hostile foreign intelligence agencies?

---

56 Peter Strzok, "Potential Qs for DD's Call," memo, January 24, 2017, Case 1:17-cr-00232-EGS, Document 188, filed April 29, 2020, p. 1, https://storage.courtlistener.com/recap/gov.uscourts.dcd.191592/gov.uscourts.dcd.191592.188.0_8.pdf.

These guys weren't just corrupt—while they were targeting Americans, they'd made America vulnerable to very dangerous actors.

On January 24, the two agents came into my office, and I offered them a seat. I recognized one of them, Joe Pientka. He had been in on some meetings early on in the campaign where we were getting intelligence briefings. When the nominees for the different big parties are selected, they start giving them copies of the President's Daily Briefs. We had the first one up in New York, and Agent Pientka was in the room at that time.

The other agent was Peter Strzok. I sure didn't know it, but at the time Strzok was sleeping with the number two lawyer at the FBI, Lisa Page. She was McCabe's general counsel. An affair like that is no small thing, and when the special counsel investigation led by Robert Mueller occurred, they tried to bury it by moving Strzok out of the spotlight. Strzok and Page also left a long trail of private text messages about the Crossfire Hurricane investigation. When they were made public, those communications gave a lot of insight into how the FBI was going after Trump and his aides. Strzok and Page told each other that they would stop Trump from becoming president and, even if he did, they had "an insurance policy."[57]

But in the January 24 meeting, Strzok and Pientka just started asking questions. I wasn't worried about anything because I had nothing to worry about. It felt like a very friendly meeting. We talked about the excitement of coming into the White House. I asked them if they had ever been in the NSA's office. It's a historic place.

In retrospect, and knowing what we all know now, it's clear they were trying to get me to lie. They started asking me questions about Ambassador Kislyak and the phone call. They asked: Did you talk about this? Do you remember this? And so forth. It was ridiculous. They knew exactly what I said because they had likely read the transcript of my conversation. I didn't have time for this.

---

57 Laura Jarrett, "Months-worth of FBI Employees' Texts Dreading Trump Victory Released to Congress," CNN, December 12, 2017, https://www.cnn.com/2017/12/12/politics/peter-strzok-texts-released/index.html

I was preparing to implement the policies of the new president, a maverick who wanted to change the way America did things in order to better serve Americans. I was talking to hundreds of people. I was dealing with issues related to Iran and its nuclear weapons program—a massive national security issue. Then there was North Korea and Little Rocket Man threatening to test nuclear weapons again. There was war in the Middle East, Afghanistan, and a hot conflict in Eastern Europe with the Ukrainians and Russian proxies shooting at each other.

I was a very busy man and didn't really have time to meet with the FBI for this—I met with them because the FBI requested it, and I had a lot of respect for what was once the world's top law enforcement agency. Unfortunately for America, that's no longer the case, and the FBI has no one to blame but themselves.

Strzok and Pientka wanted to talk to me about a phone call. I answered to the best of my ability and sent them on their way. Thanks, guys. Appreciate it. Look forward to working with you. They left, and that was it. Or that's what I thought. In fact, the get Flynn operation was about to move into a different gear.

BLOOD IN THE WATER

Pientka and Strzok knew I hadn't lied to them and went back to FBI headquarters and actually said that I hadn't.[58]

I later learned from the prosecutor eventually assigned to investigate my case that the agents did not believe I was lying at all. [59] And

---

58 *United States of America v. Michael T. Flynn*, United States District Court for the District of Columbia, Case 1:17-cr-00232-EGS, Document 198, filed May 7, 2020, p. 63, https://static1.squarespace.com/static/5e80e0d236405d1c7b8eaec9/t/5e b4b4abfa9e604b19e3cae4/1588901092641/Doc.198+Flynn+Governments++ Motion+to+DISMISS+against+Michael+T.+Flynn.pdf.

59 Olivia Beavers, "House Intel Report: McCabe Said Agents Who Interviewed Flynn 'Didn't Think He Was Lying,'" *The Hill*, May 4, 2018, https://thehill.com/policy/ national-security/386323-house-intel-report-comey-mccabe-testified-that-the-two-agents-who/.

it's because they knew I wasn't lying that they had to falsify evidence to frame me.[60]

FBI investigators memorialize their interviews in a document referred to as a (Form) 302. These records are supposed to be completed soon after the interview to ensure the notes accurately record the interview and the agents' impressions before their memory begins to fade. Hard as it is to believe, even in the twenty-first century, the FBI rarely records these interviews electronically—which makes you wonder if they're intentionally designed to give the FBI leeway to insert data that doesn't belong in an official document. That was certainly so in my case.

Violating FBI and DOJ protocol, Strzok gave the 302 of his interview with me to his lover Lisa Page, McCabe's general counsel, to rewrite.[61] They wanted to ensure it was worded correctly so the DOJ could use it in their campaign against me. Then they shuffled the 302 around to various offices at the FBI headquarters over the next several months to hide it. To this day, no one outside the FBI team that targeted me has seen the original 302. You have to wonder, where is it?

Two days after my meeting with Strzok and Pientka, Acting Attorney General Sally Yates went to 1600 Pennsylvania Avenue to meet with White House Counsel Don McGahn. She told him that I might have misled Pence.[62] Worse, according to this career bureaucrat, since the Russians knew that there were discrepancies between

---

60 "Exhibit 5: FBI Counterintelligence Investigations," March 2, 2017, Case 1:17-cr-00232-EGS, Document 198-6, filed May 7, 2020, p. 8, https://storage.courtlistener.com/recap/gov.uscourts.dcd.191592/gov.uscourts.dcd.191592.198.6.pdf, p8.

61 *United States of America v. Michael T, Flynn,* Case 1:17-cr-00232-EGS, Document 198-6, filed May 7, 2020, p. 79, https://static1.squarespace.com/static/5e80e0d236405d1c7b8eaec9/t/5eb4b4abfa9e604b19e3cae4/1588901092641/Doc.198+Flynn+Governments++Motion+to+DISMISS+against+Michael+T.+Flynn.pdf; Cristina Laila, "BREAKING: Flynn Lawyers Reveal FBI Attorney Lisa Page Edited Flynn FBI Report—Then Lied to DOJ about Edits," *Gateway Pundit,* October 24, 2019, https://www.thegatewaypundit.com/2019/10/breaking-lisa-page-edited-flynn-fbi-302-report-then-lied-to-doj-about-edits/.

62 "A Timeline of Sally Yates' Warnings to the White House about Mike Flynn," ABC News, May 8, 2017, https://abcnews.go.com/Politics/timeline-sally-yates-warnings-white-house-mike-flynn/story?id=47272979.

what Kislyak and I had discussed and what I supposedly told Pence, I might be vulnerable to blackmail.

I am trying to imagine how any adult could take that reasoning at face value. The facts are simple enough: I knew what I said, the Russians knew what I said, and the FBI knew what I said. The only apparent weak link was Pence, who panicked (or not) on a Sunday morning talk show and talked to a hostile press corps when he should have known better. The point is that there were no grounds for blackmail.

The White House counsel should have thrown her out of his office, and the fact he didn't raises a crucial issue. The Trump team as I've mentioned many times was unseasoned. We weren't Beltway insiders, which is why the American people put Donald J. Trump in the White House to begin with. The electorate chose us to "drain the swamp," as the president had said repeatedly on the campaign trail. And yet so many people in that White House seemed to be in awe of the swamp and its gruesome swamp creatures, like Yates. All McGahn and others had to do was remember who was elected to run the government, thank the bureaucrats for their input, take their advice or ignore it, and get back to work on behalf of the president and the people who elected him.

That's what Pence should have done, too. Instead, he willingly assisted the FBI's Get Flynn operation.

McCabe went to the White House to brief Pence's staff on February 10—a briefing timed to another leak of classified intelligence.[63] The day before, the same Adam Entous who'd passed on the initial leak of my call with Kislyak published key parts of the intercept.

Later we found out that Strzok and his girlfriend, Lisa Page, traded text messages about using briefings of the transition team

63 Tim Hains, "Reince Priebus Recalls Meeting Andrew McCabe at White House," RealClearPolitics, February 4, 2018, https://www.realclearpolitics.com/video/2018/02/04/reince_priebus_recalls_meeting_andrew_mccabe_at_white_house.html.

and then the new White House staff to spy on the president and his aides. One exchange refers to sending a counterintelligence agent ("CI guy") to "assess if there [*sic*] are any news [*sic*] Qs, or different demeanor. If Katie's husband is there, he can see if there are people we can develop for potential relationships."[64]

The "Katie" they refer to appears to be an FBI agent who worked in counterintelligence under Strzok, Katherine Seaman. Her husband was Pence's chief of staff, Josh Pitcock. Pitcock released a statement saying there was no "infiltration" through him or his wife. Pence told the media he "was deeply offended to learn that two disgraced FBI agents considered infiltrating our transition team by sending a counterintelligence agent to one of my very first intelligence briefings."

The point is that the FBI saw Pence's office as a point of attack to target Trump—and me.

When McCabe showed up at the White House on February 10, Pence called him into his office with Priebus and McGahn. They were watching TV news coverage of the leaked intercept. They told McCabe they wanted to see what he had on Flynn, and Pence lost his composure. "This is totally opposite," said Pence. "It's not what he said to me."

Pence could've confronted me, but he never did. I actually confronted him in the archway of the entrance to Priebus's office in the White House. I told Pence (again), I didn't lie to him, nor did I talk about sanctions with Kislyak, nor did I lie to the FBI agents. He looked at me with his typical smirk-type grin and then replied, that he and his wife had prayed about it. I thought that was the end of it. I believe it was at this stage that he and Priebus went to President Trump and told him what they had seen in the news was the opposite of what I had told Pence and that they believed it showed I lied to Pence. Again, I told Pence I never discussed sanctions because I didn't. Instead, he took the word of inside the Beltway knife fighters,

---

64 Jack Crowe, "Pence Lashes Out at Strzok, Page for Talk of 'Infiltrating' His Transition Team," Yahoo!News, April 26, 2019, https://www.yahoo.com/news/pence-lashes-strzok-page-talk-181757695.html?guccounter=1.

from Ignatius to McCabe, instead of trusting a vital member of the president's own team. Or maybe Pence, along with the FBI and the establishment, just seized the opportunity to push one maverick out of the White House with their sights on the maverick in the Oval Office, President Donald J. Trump.

I don't know who else had the president's ear in the Oval Office during my final meeting as NSA with Trump, where he accepted my resignation. Present were Jared Kushner and Steve Bannon. They said nothing. Trump and I exchanged some kind words between each other. I could tell he was not happy about the entire episode; he was obviously listening to his VPOTUS more than to me. At the end, Trump stood and walked to the side of the Resolute desk where I was standing, and we exchanged a man hug moment. I thanked him and offered him one warning before I left. I warned Trump about Andrew McCabe, then deputy director of the FBI. He had no idea who I was talking about at the time. After my departure, he certainly did. I firmly believe Priebus and Pence were part of my demise. Once I was gone, they thought they could better control President Trump and assist efforts to undercut his presidency, to ensure the establishment got him under control. I believe they thought that if I left the White House, the Russia thing would blow over—or as I suspect from what I learned subsequently about those inside of Pence's staff, they were part of the effort to "get Flynn to get Trump." But with my departure on February 13, as Devin Nunes put it, now there was blood in the water. As he warned them, they'd soon be gone, too, and that is exactly what happened.

CHAPTER 11

AFTERSHOCKS

INVESTIGATOR NUNES

Less than a month after I left the White House, the president was made aware that he'd been spied on by the outgoing administration. In a series of Tweets posted on March 4, 2017, Trump wrote:

> *Terrible! Just found out that Obama had my "wires tapped" in Trump Tower just before the victory. Nothing found. This is McCarthyism!*
>
> *Is it legal for a sitting President to be "wiretapping" a race for president prior to an election? Turned down by court earlier. A NEW LOW!*
>
> *I'd bet a good lawyer could make a great case out of the fact that President Obama was tapping my phones in October, just prior to Election!*
>
> *How low has President Obama gone to tap my phones during the very sacred election process. This is Nixon/Watergate. Bad (or sick) guy!*

Trump was right. Obama's FBI had him under surveillance—the whole Trump team's communications were liable to have been swept up by the FBI under the FISA warrant the bureau illegally obtained in October. But no one knew about the FISA yet, and when Devin Nunes revealed how the FBI had used the Clinton-funded Steele dossier to spy on a presidential campaign, it became the biggest political scandal in US history.

But in March 2017, instead of getting to the truth of what happened, the media went into attack mode and said Trump was the liar. But he was right 100 percent, even about his predecessor. Barack Obama is a bad guy, and a former president who violated the laws and ethics of our constitutional republic by spying on his political opponents is despicable, too, like a tyrannical third world dictator.

A few weeks later, FBI Director James Comey revealed in a congressional hearing that the bureau had the Trump team under investigation. When lawmakers on the House Intelligence Committee asked why they hadn't been notified, Comey told them it was too sensitive to disclose. What arrogance—Comey boasted to the elected representatives of the American people that it was none of their business he was investigating a political campaign. There was more shocking stuff to come.

Late in March, Devin Nunes told the press that he'd seen evidence of the Obama administration unmasking the Trump team. And that it had nothing to do with the FBI's Russia investigation. What he meant is that the outgoing Obama team was just picking transition officials off transcripts to spy on us and leak it to the media. He said the leak of my conversation with Kislyak was one of the biggest and most highly classified information leaks in US history and that the FBI should have been knocking down doors in Washington to find out who was responsible.

"It should have been very easy to prove," Devin said about the leak of the transcript. He was speaking for the record in the film *Flynn: Deliver the Truth, Whatever the Cost*. "They must have known who leaked General Flynn's conversation with the Russian Ambassador." But the investigation was closed after Joe Biden was inaugurated in 2021.

"The idea that General Flynn was doing something wrong by speaking with the Russian ambassador is ridiculous," Devin said to the *Flynn* film team. "He was doing exactly what he should have been doing at the time. He was the incoming national security advisor. His job, his role, was to help to coordinate the President's strategy across all of government in an effort to protect America and advance U.S. interests and stay out of conflicts."

Speaking to foreign officials is the core of diplomacy, Devin explained. "It's why we have embassies around the world, for dialogue with friends and foes. General Flynn talking to the Russian ambassador is supposed to be the normal course of business. That's what should have been said by every Republican and the fake news. Of course, General Flynn was talking to the Russian ambassador, what do you expect him to do? It's his job. It's his role. And yet that was weaponized against him to make the narrative that Hillary Clinton and the Democrats made up about Russia, their wild fantasy about Russia, seem true."

Devin said that he knew it was going to lead to worse things for the Trump administration when I left the White House. "I said after Flynn resigned that there'd be blood in the water," says Devin. "That's what I told Reince Priebus and others. I didn't speak with General Flynn at the time because I figured he was inundated."

(Priebus never relayed this conversation to me. Sitting here now with all I've learned, that is not surprising. However, did he relay it to Pence? Someone needs to ask him.)

Devin then went on to say, "If I had, I'd have told [Flynn] not to resign. And I told them in the White House that once Flynn resigns, all you guys will go. And that's exactly what happened. Within a year, they were all gone, all the kinds of top advisors around the President, from Priebus to Bannon. I knew from the night that Flynn resigned that things would get bad because I knew they wouldn't stop with Flynn."

Devin said that one of the challenges facing President Trump was that he had a vision of how Washington, DC, worked that wasn't necessarily how it worked in practice. "He thought that many people he brought on with good resumes would do the honorable thing and do the job," said Devin. "But a lot of them were susceptible to the D.C. fake news establishment. A lot of those people don't realize just how tied that D.C. news establishment is to the Democratic Party. They still don't know it. Many of my best friends in Congress still, to this day, continue to talk to the fake news."

The coup against Trump is a dark chapter in American history, Devin said. A big part of why we made the *Flynn* film and asked people like Devin to speak with the crew is to document what happened. "It has to be part of what is taught in the American school system," Devin said. "Kids should learn from a young age just how dark this chapter of American history is. Otherwise, how are we going to have a successful country when we frame a man who wasn't just innocent but was also one of the top Generals of our era? You turn the intelligence apparatus and the justice system against someone of the caliber of General Flynn?"

According to Devin, as bad as all of Russiagate was for the country, the persecution of me and my family stands out. "No one was spared by the left when they decided to prosecute and go after their political enemies," said Devin. They went so far as to target a retired, high-level, well-respected American General and accuse him of the unthinkable—committing treason against his country."

DINNER WITH TUCKER

At the same time in March that Devin was beginning to unravel how the plot against Trump started, there were several media campaigns targeting me. First was a fake *Wall Street Journal* story about the February 2014 dinner at Cambridge University. It claimed I hadn't disclosed my contact with a Cambridge graduate student who had both British and Russian citizenship, Svetlana Lokhova.[65] The point of the story was to insinuate that I'd had some inappropriate relationship with a Russian agent, but as I already explained, the whole thing was ludicrous.

At first, my family was really upset and confused. My brother Jack called up Svetlana and asked for her side of the story. She went

65 Catherine Herridge, "Russian Academic Linked to Flynn Denies Being Spy, Says Her Past Contact Was 'Used' to Smear Him," Fox News, April 5, 2019, https://www.foxnews.com/politics/russian-academic-linked-to-flynn-denies-being-spy-says-used-to-smear-him.

LIEUTENANT GENERAL MICHAEL T. FLYNN, U.S. ARMY (RETIRED)

through a very hard time with all the garbage dumped on her by the media, US officials, and British academic circles. My family was very supportive of this young mother whose life had been turned upside down.

And it was terrible at home, too, especially for Lori. She knew it wasn't true, but it was tough for her when all this stuff was in the papers. She said that these bastards were going to go to no end to ruin our life and ruin our family's life. She was right.

The media did not care about, nor did it have any compassion for, the extended families of the Flynns and the Andrades, Lori's family. Between the two families, we have close to seventy-five siblings, nieces, nephews, children, and grandchildren as well as many more aunts, uncles, and cousins. The media didn't give a damn about perpetrating this lie no matter how much personal damage it did to me or my immediate family. It was another assassination by narrative.

Here we were, two kids from a small working-class New England town, where we grew up, met, and fell in love. We had spent decades in the military sacrificing all sorts of things because we loved our country and saw it as a blessing that we had the strength as a family to protect America—and now the media is accusing me of being a Russian spy and having an affair with a Russian woman! It was all based on a lie, and the media and the Obama cronies in the media knew it was a lie but continued to push this narrative for years.

The next week the same newspaper ran the story claiming that the Flynn Intel Group's Turkish client Ekim Alptekin and I plotted to kidnap the Turkish Muslim leader Fethullah Gülen[66] and drag him back to Turkey. The story as I mentioned before was sourced to former CIA Director James Woolsey. So, it was the same reckless institutions that were the engines of Russiagate from the outset—current and former senior intelligence officials and their media thugs.

---

66   Julian Borger, "Ex-Trump Aide Flynn Investigated over Plot to Kidnap Turkish Dissident—Report," *The Guardian,* November 10, 2017, https://www.theguardian. com/us-news/2017/nov/10/michael-flynn-trump-turkish-dissident-cleric-plot.

I wondered at the time how anyone could have published a story so nonsensical—a former American intelligence chief plotting to kidnap a US person out of the country and send him to a foreign nation? But that wasn't the point. It didn't have to make sense. In fact, the more outrageous, the better. They kept piling up the lies to pressure me—who knew what kind of twisted fantasy was coming next? The point was to break me until I had no choice but to turn on the president I'd served, Donald J. Trump.

But not all the press bought into it. There were some reporters, mostly conservatives, who saw right through it. There was also a large group of citizen journalists on social media who kept finding important documents and other information that told the truth and was helpful to me and my family. I called them an army of digital soldiers—they saw through all the fake news and reported the truth. I'm thankful for all their hard work because they were, and still are, one of the bright spots in a dark and perilous time for our country.

So was Tucker Carlson, maybe the most influential journalist of his generation, a really fearless guy who calls out the Deep State and our corrupt ruling class at every opportunity. During the middle of it all, I had dinner with Tucker. He had invited me to his place in Maine for a taping for his show. It was a great evening. At one point we realized that he attended a private high school, St. George's, in Middletown, Rhode Island, where I grew up. It was right up the street from where I lived.

We spoke about the media; the poisonous political culture of Washington, DC; and the intelligence agencies. I didn't know that while Tucker was in college he had applied to work at the CIA. It's because he believed in the country, he told me.

And now the role of the CIA and other agencies is to work with the media to shape public perception of world events. He's no outsider speculating on what goes on inside the halls of power in the nation's capital. Even before he started as a journalist, his father was one too. His father worked at ABC and then worked for the government. Tucker said that the agencies shape news coverage of world events. And the more significant the world event, the more meaningful it is, and the more aggressively they shape it. He's right.

Most of the media is based in New York but is still controlled by their Washington bureaus. The news is coming from Washington and shaped by the bureaucracies, especially the intelligence agencies. And the Washington reporters, Tucker said, "are instinctively sympathetic to the people in power rather than instinctively antagonistic. The job of a journalist is to be skeptical of government, but Washington news bureaus," he said, "are aligned with the people who are lying to us, who have every incentive to lie to us and to hide from us what they're actually doing. That's terrifying because it means that the big power centers are all on one side against the population. That's not a democracy. That's an oligarchy. And for someone like me who grew up in a different system, it's bewildering. I can hardly believe it."

He said when you can turn on the news and all you see is "an endless parade of former federal law enforcement or intelligence officials paid to come on the air to analyze politics, then you know that this organization has been captured by those agencies. I mean, these are not just former government employees. These are people with active security clearances. So, they are in continuous communication with their former colleagues at these agencies. And, so, they are acting effectively as spokesmen for these federal agencies, and they're on the air as news analysts. I cannot think of a more perverse system. And it does sort of make you worry a little bit because the point of propaganda is that you don't know you're consuming it. It's supposed to be sophisticated enough that you're fooled. But when they start putting Andrew McCabe on TV as a news analyst and paying him for that, they're not even hiding what they're doing. They don't even care if you know what they're doing. They're doing it anyway. And that suggests they believe they have so much power, they don't have to convince you. At that point, they've ripped off the mask."

Tucker said he heard about what was happening to me during the first days of the Trump administration, and when he started to think about it more, it revealed what's gone wrong with our society.

In Washington, he says, the liars are exalted, and the truth tellers are punished.

Tucker told me that after the dinner, he went home and went to take his dogs out and collapsed, blowing out two of his discs, which required surgery. And then he said, "I'm not a doctor. I don't think anyone can know. But that dinner was so shocking to me. That was a pivot point, really, in my understanding of how the world works, that I honestly think it blew these two discs in my back."

What we discussed during that three-hour dinner included not only the things I experienced during my persecution but also the things I witnessed during my time as a senior intelligence officer working at the highest levels of the US intelligence community (USIC) , all during the Obama administration. I shared with Tucker insights and experiences of the way the Washington elite are captured and compromised. I also shared with him things I discovered when I started looking into the books of the USIC. There are incredible levels of waste, fraud, abuse of the system, and seriously deep levels of corruption that are destroying America and must be reformed or eliminated.

We stayed in touch and continue to speak. We live not too far from each other in Florida. Some of what we talk about was captured in the *Flynn* film, but Tucker is such an important and amazing voice at this time in our history I wanted to relay as much of our conversations as I could.

He talked about how Trump represented a threat to the Washington, DC, consensus. "The total alignment between the parties on the issues that matter," he said, "not on the minor stuff, but on the big stuff, the economy and war, the two big decisions are how do you guide the economy, and do you go to war? Those are the decisions that historians write about, not the peripheral garbage that we obsess over, but the real decisions are about the economy and war. And on those topics, there is a total alignment between the leadership of both parties."

In the wars the US fought from Vietnam starting with the Gulf of Tonkin Resolution in 1964 until now, for fifty-nine years, Tucker said, "We have never fought a war that made the U.S. stronger." The US government is now so distorted that "what's good for the United States and its population of 350 million does not enter into the equation. They had to end democracy in the United States effectively because the goal is not helping the country. The goal is preserving the institution. And in this case, the institution happens to be the U.S. government. It could be any institution. This is the nature of institutions, and this is why it's always a threat when they get too big."

Fighting that institution and the establishment is more than just a political fight—it's also sociological and spiritual because you're taking on a culture determined to preserve itself and rule the rest of the country. It's an evil idea at odds with the very principles of our constitutional republic and government by consent: It means tyranny.

"Anybody who dares to even suggest that we begin a total overhaul of that system is an enemy and will be stopped," said Tucker. "I don't believe that there's an explicit conspiracy simply because those are too complex and hard to keep secret and, in the end, not very effective. Most conspiracies fail. What succeeds is an informal alignment based on shared interests and like mind. The hivemind. If everybody in a position of authority has the same gut reactions to things as the same instincts, it's a very effective block. It's a very effective way to maintain power."

Trump was a threat to institutional Washington, which is why the establishment surrounded him with figures to keep him in line and preserve the system. Mike Pence, said Tucker, was one of the guardians of the system. "It's pretty obvious that Pence was brought in and presented to Trump," said Tucker. "I think it's very obviously an effort by Republicans in Washington, permanent Washington, to put some kind of moderating force right next to Trump. You know, you need him to win the evangelicals. That's how they sold them. And, so, they tell him, you got to have this guy. You can't win without this guy. And clearly, and I watched it firsthand, Pence believed that his role was to get Trump to go along with the conventions of Washington as it existed before Trump got there. Pence saw his job as influencing Trump to let things continue to go roughly the way they were going before."

Instead, Tucker said, Trump should have had an entire administration full of Mike Flynns. "People who wanted to set the country back on track." But I was a threat to the establishment because of my experience and my authority. And that, said Tucker, "is a massive threat to them. The average person doesn't know and has no way of knowing how many federal dollars are flowing to these intelligence agencies because it's a black budget." But I did. And because of that, Tucker said, I was, by definition, the most dangerous possible person for Donald Trump to hire.

And it's because the only real crime in the seat of the American government is telling the truth and revealing the crimes that have been committed in the name of national security, I was punished for telling the truth, not for lying.

Tucker said that one of the saddest things he's ever seen in Washington was the unwillingness of anyone in the Trump administration or Washington to defend me. But the point of course was to make me a pariah and Trump too. "The people who might have reformed the government were either repelled by Trump personally or they were too intimidated to join the administration," Tucker said. And once I was threatened with indictment, he said, "the message was really clear—you get involved with this guy, you're not paying those tuitions. You could go to jail. And what that did was prevent any competent people from signing on with that administration."

My crime, said Tucker, "was sincere patriotism. And having different views about what serves America most effectively in the foreign policy realm." The fact they were willing to literally put me in prison, said Tucker, "is so revealing of who they are. That is so dark. The idea that you'd be willing to put an innocent man in prison. Normal people would not do that. You might be annoyed by someone or, you know, Shut up, you're in the way or, you're an idiot, be quiet. But to unleash the mechanics of the U.S. justice system on someone with consequences like life imprisonment? That is ruthless."

I told Tucker that it would have been harder if it weren't for my family. Family members, he agreed, are the only people you can trust fully and who love you unequivocally. I was moved to hear him say that my story is inspiring because I wasn't broken. And because of the love of my family and my faith and the grace of God, I wasn't. And Tucker was right when he said, "[Mike Flynn, whatever you think of him], never expected to find himself in the fulcrum of history." Or to be persecuted by my own government, which I had served for the course of my entire life.

Tucker went on to say, the best we can hope for is to be surrounded by people who love and support us during such a time, and for the strength to continue through adversity. My family and I were wounded by what happened, as Tucker said, but not broken. Nor did my commitment to tell the truth ever waver.

"And," said Tucker, "if you come out of a situation like that one with that intact, you've won." That's true, but as 2017 wore on and the Justice Department threatened me and my family, I didn't feel like I was winning.

CHAPTER 12

JUSTICE BETRAYED

MUELLER UNLEASHED

After I left the White House, the media planted itself in front of our home in Northern Virginia. Vans, cars, cameras—you can imagine how disruptive that was not just for my family but for the whole neighborhood. It was a pain for our neighbors to deal with all the traffic, and for me and Lori, we couldn't walk outside our front door.

We used the back entrance to escape. Sometimes Lori and I would take a walk down by the Potomac River early in the morning or late at night and sneak back in. Amazingly, the media never caught on that there was a back entrance—it was great for us but tells you something about the nature of our press corps. It's a brainless herd without the ability to think on their own.

They also hounded my son Michael. He lived in a house in another part of Northern Virginia. It was a nice little neighborhood, with lots of young families like his. Most of the reporters who camped out in front of his place were about the same age but entirely incapable of understanding what they were putting this young father-to-be through.

Soon the Justice Department went after him too. Even though Michael had worked in an administrative capacity for the Flynn Intel Group, federal prosecutors came after him as part of their attack on me. Just because I'd left Donald Trump's government didn't mean that the get Flynn operation was over, far from it.

During transition into and while I was still at the White House, I was notified that there were issues with Flynn Intel Group's Turkey work. The DOJ said we hadn't filed the right paperwork. They were lying. They were using it as an excuse to undermine me in the performance of my duties and, as we later learned, to undermine the duly elected POTUS, President Donald J. Trump.

To represent Ekim Alptekin's company, we had first been advised in the fall of 2016 by our business lawyers to file with Congress under what's called the Lobbying Disclosure Act (LDA). And we properly and legally filed this requirement. We were not representing a foreign government or a foreign agent—unlike Hunter Biden, who made a fortune off his foreign connections.[67] Rather, we had a contract with a company owned by a foreigner, Ekim. Former senator, and vice presidential candidate, Joe Lieberman did the same thing when he filed under the LDA to represent the Chinese telecommunications giant ZTE, even though that company has known ties to the Chinese military. The DOJ was just targeting us to undermine me and then-Candidate Trump.

Either way, DOJ said Flynn Intel Group needed to file papers under the Foreign Agents Registration Act, the 1938 law requiring anyone representing a foreign government or agent to register with the Department of Justice. Yes, Ekim had ties with Turkish government officials but didn't represent the Ankara government. As proven later during the DOJ's case against my former business partner Bijan Rafiekian[68] and the case the Mueller team was trying to make against me, Ekim's payments to Flynn Intel Group came from his company. So why were we singled out? Two reasons.

First is that our consulting work eventually came to focus on Fethullah Gülen, the Turkish Islamist who'd been living in the US for more than two decades. I didn't really know much about him prior to this. But when we started looking, we found a lot of shady stuff. I mentioned before that he had a network of schools across the

---

67 Miranda Devine, *Laptop from Hell: Hunter Biden, Big Tech, and the Dirty Secrets the President Tried to Hide* (New York and Nashville, TN: Post Hill Press, 2021), https://www.amazon.com/Laptop-Hell-Hunter-Secrets-President/dp/163758105X.

68 "DOJ Drops Long-Running Court Case against Akin Client Bijan Rafiekian," Akin Gump Strauss Hauer & Feld LLP, press release, September 12, 2023, https://www.akingump.com/en/insights/press-releases/doj-drops-long-running-court-case-against-akin-client-bijan-rafiekian.

US that imports teachers to our country, but he also had schools all over the world with teachers that are loyal to him and the Gülenist movement.[69] In other words, Gülen was head of an enormous Islamist movement with operatives planted in foreign countries around the world that made him head of what is effectively an intelligence organization.[70] Inside Turkey itself, members of Gülen's massive movement played key roles in the police and eventually the army. And that's one reason why the Turks believe Gülen masterminded[71] their 2016 coup attempt.[72]

The Turkish government also accused the CIA of playing a role in the failed coup. I have no idea whether that's true, but the fact is that there's long been tension between the US and fellow NATO member Turkey. It's possible that some US intelligence officials saw Gülen as an ace in the hole. If something were to go wrong in Turkey, he'd be their guy.

I think that's one reason the DOJ went after the Flynn Intel Group for its work on Turkey. And there's another, maybe more important, issue. The DOJ's FARA unit is under the National Security Division, which is basically an intelligence agency on its own. At the time, a man named David Laufman was in charge of its counterintelligence section, where he came up with the idea of using FARA to target the Trump campaign.[73]

69 Yetkin Yildirim, "The Educator and the School in Fethullah Gülen's Educational Model," Gulen Movement, n.d., https://www.gulenmovement.com/the-educator-and-the-school-in-fethullah-gulens-educational-model.html.
70 Asli Aydintasbas, "The Good, the Bad, and the Gülenists," European Council on Foreign Relations, September 23, 2016, https://ecfr.eu/publication/the_good_the_bad_and_the_gulenists7131/.
71 "Gülen Movement," Wikipedia, https://en.wikipedia.org/wiki/Gülen_movement.
72 Peter Beaumont, "Fethullah Gülen: Who Is the Man Turkey's President Blames for Coup Attempt?" *The Guardian*, July 16, 2016, https://www.theguardian.com/world/2016/jul/16/fethullah-gulen-who-is-the-man-blamed-by-turkeys-president-for-coup-attempt.
73 Paul Sperry, "No Evidence Needed for Collusion Probe, Just a Pretext Devised by This Man," RealClearInvestigations, June 19, 2020, https://www.realclearinvestigations.com/articles/2020/06/23/no_evidence_needed_for_collusion_probe_just_an_obscure_pretext_spearheaded_by_this_man_124020.html.

In fact, the fake counterintelligence investigation known as Crossfire Hurricane was all based on FARA. Carter Page was the only one under investigation for his supposed ties to Russia. George Papadopoulos was investigated for his alleged connections to Israel; Paul Manafort was targeted for his work with Ukrainian officials; Trump campaign adviser Walid Phares was investigated for his alleged relationship with Egypt; and I was investigated for mine with Turkey. In other words, the DOJ's case against me for my company's work with Ekim was a continuation of Crossfire Hurricane.

Of course, I didn't know at the time that I was under an FBI investigation or that the pretext was Flynn Intel Group's contract with a Turkish businessman. So, when the DOJ started sending me letters warning me to retain records of the Turkey work, I was a little rattled. The lawyer I'd used to write consulting contracts told me that FARA wasn't a big deal and I'd probably just have to register with DOJ. For the administrative process, she suggested that I use Covington & Burling, an enormous global firm with an office in Washington, DC, where numerous former US officials hang out their shingles. The firm's senior partners include Obama's former attorney general and "wingman" Eric Holder and Michael Chertoff, former secretary of Homeland Security under the Bush and Obama administrations. That probably should have warned me away from Covington, but at the time I still had faith in the law and knew we had done nothing wrong.

In the meantime, things were not going great back at the White House. There were more leaks, like transcripts of calls with foreign leaders, and Trump asked Comey to look into it. It makes us look terrible to have these things leaking, Trump told him. The president also talked about the leak of my conversation with Kislyak and said I hadn't said anything wrong in my call with the Russian ambassador. During a dinner with Comey, Trump told him that he hoped he could let it go.

After Trump finally fired the FBI director, a move long overdue, Comey leaked Trump's comments about me to the press in the hope of getting a special counsel appointed. The FBI wanted to frame Trump for obstructing the Russia investigation. And Comey's ploy worked. On May 17, 2017, the DOJ named Robert Mueller special counsel to investigate Russian interference in the election. In other words, the special counsel was also a continuation of the Crossfire Hurricane investigation.

And with that, Mueller's team came after me for violating FARA. I'd thought that my Covington lawyers had resolved the problem but no way. I paid them $300,000. Not only did they not fix the FARA issue, but they wound up effectively on the side of the special counsel.[74] At this point, I started to realize the problem wasn't administrative paperwork—the Deep State was hunting me.

My Covington lawyers asked if I had anything on Trump to give the special counsel. I couldn't believe they expected me to turn on the president, who had done nothing wrong. But throughout the summer and fall Mueller's team turned up the heat on me by leaking to the press that they were considering charging Michael.[75]

So, if I didn't want to invent something about Trump, and if I didn't want to see my son targeted by federal law enforcement, I had to plead guilty for making false statements to the FBI in my January 24 White House interview with Peter Strzok and Joe Pientka. Except I didn't lie to the FBI. I asked my lawyers to obtain the 302 and any

74 Joe Hoft, "After Years of Hiding Emails from General Flynn, His Former Attorneys at Covington—Where Obama's 'Wingman' Is Partner—Suddenly Discover Thousands of Documents Related to Case," *Gateway Pundit*, April 29, 2020, https://www.thegatewaypundit.com/2020/04/years-hiding-emails-general-flynn-former-attorneys-covington-law-firm-obamas-wingman-partner-suddenly-discovers-thousands-documents-related-case/; Joe Hoft, "BREAKING EXCLUSIVE: General Flynn's First Law Firm Hired Deep State FBI Attorney at Same Time They Were Repping Flynn—Did They Share with Flynn This Conflict of Interest?" *Gateway Pundit*, January 18, 2020, https://www.thegatewaypundit.com/2020/01/breaking-exclusive-general-flynns-first-law-firm-hired-deep-state-fbi-attorney-at-same-time-they-were-repping-flynn-did-they-share-with-flynn-this-conflict-of-interest/;   C. Ryan Barber, *National Law Journal*, "Covington Hands Over More Files to Mike Flynn, After 'Inadvertently' Missing Them Earlier," April 9, 2020, https://www.law.com/nationallawjournal/2020/04/09/covington-hands-over-more-files-to-mike-flynn-after-inadvertently-missing-them-earlier/?slreturn=20250112-30555.
75 Carol E. Lee, Julia Ainsley, and Ken Dilanian, "Mike Flynn's Son Is Subject of Federal Russia Probe," NBC News, September 13, 2017, https://www.nbcnews.com/news/us-news/mike-flynn-s-son-subject-federal-russia-probe-n800741.

notes from the interview, but Mueller's prosecutors initially refused to hand them over. Prior to pleading guilty, I was finally shown a 302 to read (with no notes), but to this day the original 302 has still not been reviewed by me. The one I read my lawyers advised they could get a guilty plea because of the way the 302 was written. After the fact, I learned along with the rest of the country, that there were so many changes and so many hands that illegally touched this 302, that my guess is the original 302 was destroyed, another crime committed by the FBI.[76]

The prosecutor in charge of my case was Brandon Van Grack. I recall first meeting him in November 2017, and my lawyers told me afterward that it didn't go well, and I could get fifteen years in prison.

I thought to myself, what bastards. I've been overseas on six continents to serve my country. I've served years in combat and fought wars to protect America—and before most of these swamp creatures were even born. Van Grack was tremendously arrogant, a perfect specimen of the type of person who comes to Washington, DC, certain that they were born to rule over us, We the people.

Van Grack was corrupt too.[77] His DOJ and FBI cohorts were spying on the Trump team and then tried to frame me and the president. He'd obtained emails of the Trump transition team that were privileged communications and failed to disclose that the special counsel team had accessed those privileged materials. Van Grack also made

---

76 Sundance, "Strzok Fired, Likely Bruce Ohr Is Next—False FISA Affidavits, Fraudulent 302s, Security Clearances Under Review…," The Last Refuge, August 15, 2018, https://theconservativetreehouse.com/blog/2018/08/15/strzok-fired-likely-bruce-ohr-is-next-false-fisa-affidavits-fraudulent-302s-security-clearances-under-review/; *United States of America v. Michael T. Flynn*, United States District Court, District of Columbia, Case 1:17-cr-0232-EGS, Document 160, filed January 29, 2020, p. 1, Wayback Machine, https://web.archive.org/web/20200303031900/https://sidneypowell.com/wp-content/uploads/2020/01/Completed-ECF-160-with-Attachments.pdf.

77 Joe Hoft, "Corrupt DOJ and Mueller Attorney Van Grack Committed Many False and Fraudulent Activities in Efforts to Indict General Flynn," *Gateway Pundit*, November 30, 2019, https://www.thegatewaypundit.com/2019/11/corrupt-doj-and-mueller-attorney-van-grack-committed-many-false-and-fraudulent-activities-in-efforts-to-indict-general-flynn/.

use of an email from Trump's lawyer John Dowd to my lawyers to make it sound like there was some conspiracy between me and the White House. Dowd later commented that it was "unfair and despicable. It was a friendly privileged phone call between counsel—with NO conflict. I think Flynn got screwed."[78]

He brought charges against my business partner Bijan for the Turkey project and listed my son Michael as a potential witness to intimidate me. Then, despite the fact that the DOJ asserted Bijan was acting as a foreign agent for Turkey, Van Grack never investigated nor appeared to care whether or not the agreement with Ekim's company was funded by the Turkish government. It was not, and he knew it from the beginning. And when it came to the FBI case against me, the DOJ's documents showed that Van Grack mixed up Peter Strzok and Joe Pientka.[79] Van Grack was in such a hurry to frame me and give Trump a black eye, the facts didn't matter.[80]

I asked my lawyers to find out if Strzok and Pientka thought that I lied. I didn't know at the time that they'd told Comey and McCabe they thought I hadn't lied.[81] But I knew that I didn't lie, so I wanted to know what they believed.

78 Techno Fog (@Techno_Fog), X (formerly Twitter), November 30, 2019, X thread accessed on Thread Reader, https://threadreaderapp.com/thread/1200584606803775493.html.

79 Adam Mill, "As the Flynn Case Disintegrates, Parallels with Ukraine Emerge," American Greatness, November 7, 2019, https://amgreatness.com/2019/11/07/as-the-flynn-case-disintegrates-parallels-with-ukraine-emerge/.

80 Rachel Weiner, "Michael Flynn Reviewed FARA Filing He Later Called False, Ex-Lawyer Testifies," *Washington Post*, July 16, 2019, https://www.washington-post.com/local/public-safety/michael-flynns-ex-lawyer-testifies-on-the-former-na-tional-security-advisers-consulting-work/2019/07/16/f317b28a-a801-11e9-86dd-d7f0e60391e9_story.html; Jeremy B. White, "Michael Flynn's Son a Target of Robert Mueller's Trump-Russia Investigation, Says Report," *The Independent* (US Edition), September 13, 2017, https://www.independent.co.uk/news/world/americas/us-politics/michael-flynn-son-trump-russia-investigation-mueller-target-latest-a7945496.html; Matthew Barakat, "Prosecutors Drop Charges against Bijan Kian, a Onetime Business Partner of Michael Flynn," AP, September 11, 2023, https://apnews.com/article/rus-sia-bijan-kian-turkey-flynn-dropped-charges-5d28d5f09b8b5dcdb44fabef39ec1543.

81 Peter Strzok, "Potential Qs for DD's Call," memo, Case 1:17-cr-00232-EGS, Document 188, filed April 29, 2020, January 24, 2017, https://static1.squarespace.com/static/5e80e0d236405d1c7b8eaec9/t/5eab5945318c6f3c3787f75f/1588287820116/ECF-No.-188.pdf.

There was so much I didn't know because the DOJ had hidden it all. I didn't know that Strzok's lover Lisa Page had rewritten the original 302[82] to frame me, and I also didn't know they were hiding that original somewhere, so when my lawyers told me and Lori that the FBI "agents stand by their statements," it was time for me to make one of the biggest decisions in my life.[83]

We'd already spent an unholy amount of money on my defense. I thought to myself that I had to stop the bleeding. It wasn't just the financial cost; there was also the emotional bleeding. It was hurting my wife, my kids, and my family. Had I decided to fight, I'd find myself in front of a Washington, DC, jury that was primed to hate me, my family, Trump, and the White House. Could I even hope to get a fair trial there?

Plus, my son [was?] would have been next on their hit list. Those bastards wouldn't stop until they chewed off every piece of meat on my body, like piranhas. It was hard enough that I could barely speak with Michael. My lawyers told me I had to communicate with him through them. It was hell.

They were going after my son, and I could not let that happen. Every time I put on our country's uniform I was prepared to give my life for this country. There's nothing I wouldn't give to protect my family. My other son, Matthew, was working in South Korea for the government at the time, and one time they tried to go after him, too. But I wasn't going to let any of that happen.

There were times I thought about my mother and father in their last days, and I wished that I could have been there to hug them and

---

82 *United States of America v. Michael T. Flynn*, United States District Court for the District of Columbia, Case 1:17-cr-00232-EGS, Document 198, filed May 7, 2020, p.79, https://static1.squarespace.com/static/5e80e0d236405d1c7b8eaec9/t/5eb4 b4abfa9e604b19e3cae4/1588901092641/Doc.198+Flynn+Governments++Motion +to+DISMISS+against+Michael+T.+Flynn.pdf.

83 *United States of America v. Michael T. Flynn*, United States District Court, District of Columbia, Case 1:17-cr-00232-EGS, Document 129, filed October 24, 2019, p. 31, https://storage.courtlistener.com/recap/gov.uscourts.dcd.191592/gov. uscourts.dcd.191592.129.0_1.pdf.

say, "I love you and everything's going to be okay." It was the same with Michael. He and his wife had just had a baby, my grandson. I wanted to hug them all and tell him it's going to be okay because I'm here for you. These bastards thought they caught him in their trap, but they weren't going to touch my son.

So, the night of November 30, I started calling my brothers and sisters. My decision was going to affect them and everyone else I loved. Lori's brothers and sisters, in-laws, people from Middletown, everyone I knew. They knew me as a military officer, the director of the DIA, national security advisor to the commander-in-chief of the greatest country in world history, but they also knew me as a brother, a son, a husband, a father, and a citizen. I wanted to explain how I'd come to my decision.

I am not going to say that I wasn't depressed, but I'm not some-one who holds on to hate. Hate will just tear you apart. Hate is the natural reaction for people who feel like the world has turned against them, and they have no power in their lives, and that's not me. I act to make my life better and my family's life better. I served in the Army to make our country better and to protect and preserve our peace and prosperity, so when something bad happens and a problem arises, I try to figure out how to fix it.

Lori and I sat down, and I discussed with my wife how I was going to fix this. We've known each other since we were thirteen years old, and she's always been my rock. No matter how bad things got, she'd say, "Don't we always have each other?" And it's true that when you're with somebody you deeply love, and they love you back like that, you know that everything's going to be okay in the end. But I also had to deal with what has happening right then, in the present.

The worst part for her was the night I made my calls to tell every-one I'd come to a decision. I was telling our loved ones that I was going to have to say something that wasn't true. This was the only way to make it end. We had no choice. The next day, we went to court, and I pled guilty to a crime I didn't commit. It was hard enough for me, but maybe even harder for Lori, my wife and best friend, who had to see me do it.

MY WIFE, THE GENERAL

For more than a year after pleading guilty, I'd been cooperating with the Department of Justice on a case where the prosecutors had no evidence on anyone. They probably thought just the fact I was identified as a cooperating witness would unnerve the White House. I assumed that, but regardless of how often they wanted me to make things up about Trump, I refused. Van Grack and another DOJ attorney assigned to my case, as well as members of the Mueller team who sat down with me from time to time, such as Andrew Weismann, grew increasingly frustrated.

On December 18, 2018, a little more than a year after I pled guilty, I appeared before Judge Emmet Sullivan for my sentencing hearing. My lawyers and my wife and I met at their firm's headquarters for us to proceed to the courthouse that day, and the DOJ sent dozens of lawyers, including the solicitor general, himself. The courtroom was packed and so was the overflow room, jammed with national and international media. I was told by one of the security guards at the courthouse, whom I had come to know, this was the most people and journalists this courthouse ever had attend a hearing. My lawyers told me not to worry because I wouldn't have to say much. They told me that they and the prosecutor, Van Grack, had previously spoken and that he was going to do most of the talking.

Again, my lawyers showed they didn't know what they were talking about because the judge took control and started peppering me with questions I wasn't ready for. But maybe there's no way anyone could've been ready for what Sullivan had in store.

He pointed to the flag and then turned to accost me on the charge I had pled guilty to, lying to the FBI, and also for Flynn Intel Group's work for Ekim (something I wasn't being charged with). The way the media framed it, I was promoting Turkish and Russian interests as part of the Trump campaign. Sullivan either believed that stupid mischaracterization or had just joined the Deep State's propaganda campaign against me. Maybe, as some have speculated, he watched the previous night's episode of *The Rachel Maddow Show* and was parroting what she said. All of which were either lies, false innuendo he was making up on the fly, or deliberate personal attacks that clearly had no place in his courtroom and certainly should never have been said by a judge, never mind a lifetime appointed federal judge. He was way out of control that day. What makes the whole episode regarding the Turkey FARA violations even more unhinged is the fact that I have never even been to Turkey. As I wrote above, I worked with the Turkish military in Afghanistan, but I never had the opportunity to visit Turkey. So much for being a foreign agent for Turkey. During the court hearing, Judge Sullivan pressed on:

"Arguably, that undermines everything this flag over here stands for," Sullivan said. "Arguably, you sold your country out."[84]

I couldn't believe what I was hearing. No one in the courtroom or the overflow room could believe it. But it didn't end there. Sullivan asked Van Grack if what I'd done "rises to the level of treasonous activity?"[85] Then he asked Van Grack, "Could he have been charged with treason?"[86]

This was incredible. We'd filed the correct LDA paperwork to finish a project for Ekim's company, like hundreds of others in Washington, DC, who represent international business interests. But

84   "Transcript of Sentencing Proceedings Before the Honorable Emmet G. Sullivan, United States District Court Judge," *United States v. Michael Flynn*, United States District Court for the District of Columbia, Criminal Action No. 17-232, December 18, 2018, p. 33, lines 12–14, https://www.justsecurity.org/wp-content/uploads/2018/12/121818am-USA-v-Michael-Flynn-Sentencing.pdf.
85   "Transcript of Sentencing Proceedings Before the Honorable Emmet G. Sullivan, United States District Court Judge," p. 36, lines 1–2, 9–10, https://www.justsecurity.org/wp-content/uploads/2018/12/121818am-USA-v-Michael-Flynn-Sentencing.pdf 36, Lines 1-2, 9-10.
86   "Transcript of Sentencing Proceedings Before the Honorable Emmet G. Sullivan, United States District Court Judge," p. 36, lines 9–10, https://www.justsecurity.org/wp-content/uploads/2018/12/121818am-USA-v-Michael-Flynn-Sentencing.pdf.

to keep Crossfire Hurricane in play, the DOJ decided we had to file for FARA as well. So, Flynn Intel Group paid hundreds of thousands of dollars to follow the Justice Department's demands and register with them. It wasn't until years later we learned that none of these filings were necessary and that the DOJ had to dismiss its case against my former business partner Bijan due to lack of evidence. Still somehow, in the mind of Emmet Sullivan, I had committed treason. A combat veteran who had worn his country's uniform for thirty-three years had betrayed America.

I'd thought the year before that pleading guilty was going to resolve my issues and restore peace to my family. But now, my adversaries were turning reality inside out.

I took a three-by-five card and wrote "WTH!" on it and passed it to my lawyer. This was bad and heading somewhere worse. Eventually, Sullivan asked if we needed to take a break. That was a miracle.

"Yes, Your Honor," my lawyer said. The prosecution also said yes, so we took a break and left the courtroom. At this stage, the media is on a full-on frenzy, reporting that Sullivan accused me of treason. I felt like I'd been hit by a giant wave.

My lawyers, Lori, and I went into a little room inside the courthouse. The lawyers are all on their phones trying to figure out what happened and how to move forward. I could hear they were speaking on their phone to their senior partner Mike Chertoff. I could only hear one side of the conversation, and it didn't sound positive for me. My team of Covington lawyers were clearly shaken. Lori took charge. She said to my lawyers that we had to somehow get out of that courtroom that day. The judge wanted to put me in jail, and she was not going to let that happen. She knew if Sullivan gave us an opening to walk out of the courtroom, we needed to take it, because otherwise he was going to send me to jail.

That's Lori, always steady. That day, she was the General.

On the way back to the courtroom, the media pestered us for a comment—"The judge accused you of treason. Do you have anything you say?" We ignored them as we had always ignored them and walked back into the courtroom.

Maybe someone called Sullivan during the break, but he knew he'd done damage to the case. He opened by saying, "I made a statement about Mr. Flynn acting as a foreign agent in the White House," he said. He said he found out that he was wrong and that my work for Ekim ended before I entered the White House.

Sullivan also said he hadn't meant to "suggest" I'd committed treason. "Don't read too much into the questions I ask." He then turned to Van Grack and asked if there was any more cooperation that I could offer the Mueller investigation.[87] The prosecutor Van Grack said yes, there were some other things that I could help them with. That was the opening we needed to get away from the clutches of this corrupt prosecution and judge. We had the chance to leave the courtroom without any conviction or sentence, and we took it— another miracle. We walked back out through the media circus and went to my son Michael's house to recover, as a family, from the day's hearing. I believe to this day Judge Sullivan regrets his mistake and regrets allowing me to leave his courtroom instead of putting me in prison.

At Michael's home, surrounded by family, we discussed how the day had gone. It certainly didn't go the way our lawyers had told us it would go. Later that evening, when Lori and I were alone, we decided it was time to change lawyers. Now we needed to find someone else to pick up the gauntlet.

Sidney Powell had been in the courtroom that day and joined us later at Michael's. My brother Joe had met her a few months before in Dallas when he was raising money for the legal defense fund. They spoke over coffee for a few hours, and he convinced her to come to the trial. Sidney came to us as an unexpected blessing, a miracle really. In my public statement after my dismissal, I called Sidney the

---

87   "Transcript of Sentencing Proceedings Before the Honorable Emmet G. Sullivan, United States District Court Judge," p. 40, lines 6–19, https://www.justsecurity.org/wp-content/uploads/2018/12/121818am-USA-v-Michael-Flynn-Sentencing.pdf.

"guardian angel of American justice" for the way she stood on my behalf, as a beacon of light for the rule of law in America.

During our family meeting that night, my brothers and sisters were determined that the family fight as one. I told them I'd pled guilty because my lawyers said that if I went before a Washington, DC, jury, I'd end up in prison for fifteen to twenty-five years. They would then drag my son Michael into it and would likely throw him in prison as well. These were animals we were dealing with.

My family said, "Mike, we know you didn't commit these crimes. We have to fight." So, we resolved to fight. In June 2019 Sidney Powell took over my case, and in January 2020, I withdrew my guilty plea.

We had a lawyer who wanted to fight like we did, and as it turned out, we had supporters all over the place. People like Devin Nunes, Tucker Carlson, Mark Levin, and Rush Limbaugh, as well as an army of digital soldiers—and we had you, the American people.

CHAPTER 13

LETTERS FROM AMERICA

OLD FRIENDS AND NEW ONES

These extraordinary events took a toll on my whole family and community. When large powers with inexhaustible resources, like the American government, strike out against someone, they attack not just one person but your entire family as well as your extended personal and professional relationships. They attack your entire history because their goal is to destroy your whole world.

The low point was the December 18, 2018, court hearing. We got threatening letters. They all knew where I lived because I had the media right outside my door. I received all kinds of hate mail, people threatening my life and my family's lives. It's still going on today. It'll probably go on forever.

There are nuts out there who are just going to believe what they want to believe, and here are Americans who've been driven crazy by the government's lies about me, and other things, too.

But even at the worst of times, I was never alone, not by a long shot. I had Lori. The power that comes from a husband and wife who know and truly love each other is unbeatable.

I had my family, the Flynns of Tuckerman Avenue, their children, grandkids, and in-laws, and that huge community from my hometown. They knew me.

I also had my friends. Some became dearer to me during the hard times than they were before. They came through for us. Friends from the different towns and bases we'd called home over the years, friends from the military and my different commands, friends from government, and even from Washington, DC.

I also learned that some of the friends I loved—and by that, I mean someone I'd lay down my life for—did not love me back. Some whose love and loyalty I thought I had earned showed they were not my friends at all.

I never stopped loving those friends, but I was greatly disappointed. My loyalty runs deep. I stick to my friends, no matter how bad it gets. I was raised that way and raised my own children like that too—it's part of the Flynn code. Stick by your friends and fight for them hardest when it looks worse. Some I loved and fought for and fought alongside failed in their love and loyalty and may someday come to regret their vanity and weakness. True friends are made of stronger stuff.

As Thomas Paine wrote, "These are the times that try men's souls." The great philosopher and pamphleteer was writing at the start of the American Revolution when the fate of our forefathers' struggle for liberty was uncertain. George Washington's men were ready to leave the fight when Washington ordered the men to hear Paine's words. "The summer soldier and the sunshine patriot will, in this crisis, shrink from the service of his country; but he that stands it now, deserves the love and thanks of man and woman. Tyranny, like hell, is not easily conquered; yet we have this consolation with us, that the harder the conflict, the more glorious the triumph."

My family and I faced a wicked tyranny. Our souls were tried, but I had my faith, which was tested and strengthened throughout this entire ordeal. The summer soldiers and sunshine patriots had left the field of fight, but I had America in my corner.

The friends that I made along this journey were the American people. People I had never met suddenly came into my life. Thousands, then tens of thousands, then hundreds of thousands of people wrote me letters and sent us gifts, rosary beads, cards, paintings, quilts, donations to our legal defense fund, and even surfboards. I got three surfboards from absolute strangers—or people who were strangers before and are now friends.

I have hundreds of thousands more friends now than when I left the White House in February 2017. I was cursed and betrayed by the government I'd served, but in the middle of my hardest times, I was also blessed by God and by my fellow Americans. I received a miracle, courtesy of the country I love.

AMERICA'S GENERAL

The bills for my legal defense began to pile up almost immediately. After Robert Mueller was named special counsel, they called me in. And every time you get called in, you better have at least one attorney, if not several. With Washington, DC, attorneys, that's $700 an hour, minimum.

Before you know it, there's a $350,000 bill. We'd already sold our home in Virginia and knew that if this continued, we'd soon be broke. After thirty-three years of defending my country and fighting on many battlefields overseas, I found elements in my own government trying to destroy everything I held dear.

So, my siblings set up a fund to pay for my legal defense. They got some outside advice, and then help came right at the start from reporter Catherine Herridge, who was then with Fox News. She told my brother Joe that I was good to her when she was a national security reporter, so she offered to help by interviewing him about the fund. That was great exposure, and we were all really grateful to her for it.

Joe was sort of our spokesperson because I couldn't really speak for myself. He went on podcasts to spread the word and spoke with lots of conservative journalists about the fund. He also organized silent auctions. One time we had this painter named Michael Marrone, who did these beautiful portraits of me and other modern-day patriots. He is a great artist, and, over time, Michael truly earned the nickname, the "Commander's Artist." He allowed us to use his works of art in various auctions, silent and regular, which helped our legal defense fund.

Two others who helped in crucial ways were radio and TV hosts Mark Levin and the legendary Rush Limbaugh. They gave their great audiences regular updates about my case, and whenever they encouraged their armies of loyal listeners to support me and my family's fight against the corrupt justice system, the fund would surge. Both these gentlemen became friends. Mark and I stay in touch, and I miss Rush terribly, like we all do. What he and Mark did for me and my family is something I will never forget.

My sister Barbara did most of the heavy lifting and basically ran the fund out of her home in San Diego. She took the donations coming in and deposited them into the bank. The donors were also writing letters and cards along with the checks they sent. So, Barbara calls and says, "Mike, you've got to read these letters." She sent the first batch of letters, and I started reading them, and it was just so emotional. I read them aloud to Lori, and they brought tears to our eyes.

One of the first letters I received was addressed to my sister Barbara: "My heart breaks for General Flynn and his family," the woman wrote. "I wish I could give more. I will be keeping them in my prayers."

Barbara sent me another box, then another, and it became a ritual. She boxed up the letters at the end of every week and FedEx'd them to us. These Americans were pouring their hearts out to me. I read every one.

No matter how bad a week was, with the media pummeling me with lies, when that FedEx box arrived, Lori and I opened it up like a Christmas gift. We would take the letters out and read them to each other. I'd read a letter and call her over and say, "You got to read this one." She'd read one and say, "Oh, you have to read this letter." They were just great, great letters, tearjerkers, some of them.

So many Americans took the time to write me about how they felt as well as sending along their hard-earned dollars that I felt I owed it to them to respond.

I started to write letters back to everyone who wrote or shared something with me, and when I did, it seemed like the more I wrote, the more I got back. Whether it was those individuals who first wrote and continued to give or someone who was part of their network who they had motivated to write. I've written back to everyone who wrote me, which at this point is hundreds of thousands of letters and cards.

Strangers were telling me their problems. No matter how bad things were going for us, when we got another box of letters, we felt revived. Those letters renewed our faith in everything that we believed in. We realized that this is what it's all about. Forget the media. They don't know us. Forget about our false friends who never reached out to us when we needed it. Here are real people extending their hands in faith, friendship, and love. This is who the real America is.

Up until then I'd been underwater, and it felt like I was drowning. In those many thousands of letters, cards, gifts, donations, paintings, drawings—and surfboards—they sent me over the last seven years, and they keep coming to this day, the American people breathed air into my lungs.

When you're learning how to scuba dive, you have to learn how to "buddy breathe." It's an essential part of the training. It might save your life or your diving partner's. If your tank runs out or if you have a problem with it, your partner shares the demand valve on his tank so you can get to the surface safely. I'd been down under the water for a long, long time. Much longer than a person could normally survive. But the American people were down there with me helping me breathe.

I was able to rise to the surface because of the American people. What they told me in their letters was that they also needed the air. They asked for advice or told me about a loved one or a friend or even themselves who needed help.

Here I was feeling like I was drowning, but they came to me looking for strength. They were worried about the fate of the country and wanted to tell me how they felt and how much they depended on me to help them. It was an amazing feeling to learn how much trust the American people were placing in me at a time when I felt totally isolated and persecuted. I came to see that Americans felt the more I was attacked by the press or the government, the more the American people believed they, too, were being attacked.

They sent millions of prayers and asked me to keep them in my prayers. I thought I was in bad shape, but they sought me out as someone who could help them. That's what I mean by "buddy breathing"—we went through it together.

The letters came from all over the place. My son Michael did a heat map of the correspondence from inside the nation, and it showed letters coming from all fifty states. The average amount of money sent to support my family and me was around twenty-five dollars. There were some very wealthy people who sent thousands, but my sister would also receive donations of a dollar, two dollars, or five dollars; sometimes it was cash, sometimes a check.

There were people donating and writing me who were on Social Security, people who were on welfare, writing that after they paid their bills this is what they had left so they sent it. They sent their last ten dollars to donate to my defense because they believed in my innocence, they believed in me, and they believed in America.

Many of my correspondents had served in our military or had a close relative who served—a father, a grandfather, maybe a son or daughter who was still serving. And they expressed their faith in me and their disgust with our government. They'd studied my case very closely and understood exactly what it meant for the country as a whole.

One correspondent wrote about her father. "I'm sorry that you had to go through the Mueller Inquisition and lose everything. My father was a WWII vet. He was in a prisoner of war camp." This man had his freedom taken away—Americans are a great people who will risk everything for love of our country.

Another letter came from another man who saw combat. "I'm a retired veteran 21 years of service in the Army that I love," it began. "I had three combat tours in Vietnam, '66 to '69. I served with the 101st."

That was really hard duty in Vietnam. "I followed your ordeal from the beginning and knew right away you were innocent," he continued. "They attempted a coup against our duly elected president, something that is unprecedented in the history of our republic. You and others in this administration were in their way and had to be taken out. They could care less about your distinguished service.

"They are cowards. And I hope justice will prevail and they serve prison time for what they did. If they can railroad a general, none of us are immune to their treachery. They need to pay and pay dearly as a warning to anyone else who would attempt such a treasonous act."

One woman wrote, "Well, I can't do a lot, but if everyone gave some just to say we care and want justice, someday, evil will receive what it is due. We all have or had family members in the military. My husband was in at the end of the Korean War. If a country does not have a solid military, if we citizens sit back and see our Constitution and country go with the beliefs of the Democrats, holy heck! Don't lose faith. Keep strong, and you are in our prayers. Know you are respected by an American citizen."

Barbara passed on a funny note from a Marine—and if you know Marines, you know they're not the most sentimental guys. They show you they like you by ragging on you, so he asked my sister to tell me that "we could have had a place in our Marine Corps for him and that we forgive him for joining the Army." His joke brought me back to the beginning of my military career and how I almost was a Marine!

A former DIA analyst who retired to San Diego wrote to tell me he was honored to have served when I was director there. "I recognized your strong leadership, strength of character, and commitment to the defense of our nation." I was thankful for the note and glad that I'd managed to reflect the purpose of the organization's mission.

A retired Air Force officer in Utah who flew F-16s for twenty-four years wrote me a note of support for my case. He saw what was going on in our justice system and wondered which way the country was going. "Evil flourishes when good men do nothing," he wrote. He signed off as "USAF Retired, Small Business Owner, Disenfranchised American."

Americans respect the US military, the institution, and the people who serve. And I was a general in the United States Army. I served in combat. I served our country for almost three and a half decades. So, when Americans look at my time in the military and what I achieved during it and then I'm accused of having done all these things that are out of character with my record, people understand that something isn't right.

I got a letter from someone whose job was sniffing out wrong from right and telling the guilty from the innocent: "Dear General Flynn," he wrote, "I hope this note finds its way to you and that you and your family are safe. I was forced to retire as a detective from the New York City Police Department due to injuries I sustained during an undercover operation in 1990. I miss serving the people immensely, I loved the job. My family and I have followed you closely and can't believe how far it's gone. After you hired Miss Powell, our hopes were raised that she would use her great knowledge and skills to bring your case to justice. I am just writing to let you know that most of the country supports you. Please don't give up and keep your spirits up because you are innocent. My beautiful wife of 46 years, my kids, and grandchildren stand beside you. We hope your family stays strong. Thanks for your service to our great country. We know what a great voice you have been in protecting our great nation. We will be waiting anxiously for the positive outcome of your fight.

God bless you."

The message the American people were sending me was, thank you for standing up to what's happening, thank you for fighting for this nation, thank you for fighting for us. So, don't give up. Keep the faith. Keep fighting. We're with you.

I'm an eternal optimist, but there were tough days, trust me. Very, very tough days. But these people wrote me to say, you're our hero. At first, it struck me as a complete role reversal. I felt that I was in the worst possible place, and they were thanking me and sending me money. And then I was reminded that this is what friends do. When things get bad, your family and true friends bring you back to the best possible version of yourself.

As it turned out, I had friends everywhere. One time I had just taken my seat on a Southwest Airlines flight from Providence, Rhode Island, to Washington, DC, and a stewardess handed me a note on behalf of the pilot and the crew—it was written on the back of a paper napkin. "We're with you," it said. On another trip, the pilots and the stewardesses briefly held up the flight to take photos with me.

The American people were saying, you can't treat this guy like this. We're not going to allow it, and we're going to let him know that. They didn't like what was happening in Washington, DC, and all that was reflected in what was going on in my case. Americans were saying, we're going to stand with him and give to him to show how we treat the people we believe in. They were also sending a message to the people they don't believe in, those using the country for their own greedy ends, those who are tearing the country apart.

I received letters from around the world, like Slovenia, where a student wrote me to discuss the problems in his country. Like millions spread across the globe, he sees America as the world's great hope. He was worried the light of freedom was going out in America.

So was a correspondent from the Netherlands. She wrote that the situation there with their own version of the Deep State was getting desperate. "Due to the corrupt media," she wrote, "I do not know where else to turn to help." She said she was looking to me and my family for an example and to America for hope and leadership.

Lots of the letters I received were about faith, and how that's the core issue now facing us. One correspondent, Joyce from South Dakota, wrote to me about the saint my mother named me after, Michael the Archangel. He defends the faithful against the forces of evil, "powers and principalities." Joyce wrote that the war now being waged is a spiritual battle—and I agree.

Letters like that buttressed my faith. I could have said, okay, I'll tell these corrupt prosecutors whatever they wanted to hear so they'd leave me and my family alone. And I knew that since they're corrupt, if I said something, the worse it was, the more they'd like it. But making something up to help myself would have meant turning not only against myself, it would have meant turning against my family too. It would have meant turning against my community and the people I grew up with. It would have been turning against my country and what I fought for when I wore our country's uniform. And it would've been turning against what I still fight for now, as fiercely as ever. And most importantly, it would have meant never being able to look at myself in the mirror ever again. I wouldn't be able to face myself because I would have given up. And I've never been a guy who's quit something and given up.

After a while, people started adopting our family's motto—"Fight Like a Flynn." We were hurting, but people saw us as a model for family strength and unity. That's why many of the cards and letters sent to me during these last few years were addressed to me and Lori together.

One correspondent wrote to wish us a Merry Christmas and a Happy New Year. "I would like to tell you that your faith and courage are so encouraging to me," she wrote. "You and your family are true warriors for God and our country. I certainly learned how to 'Fight like a Flynn.'"

A husband and wife wrote to our whole family: "God bless each of you for showing America the beautiful strength of your family unity and your faith. We pray that the Flynn family will be able to celebrate an end to the outrageous persecution of America's general."

A woman wrote explaining that she and her retired US Army husband are on a very limited income but "felt we must stand with Lt Gen Flynn and his family." She wanted to convey "how much we appreciate his and his family's sacrifices to and for our country."

We Americans know that it's all about family. And it's a powerful thing when we see a family stick together and gather strength from each other. Of course, not everyone goes through what we did, facing down a corrupt justice system and a vicious media. But we all go through very tough times.

I got a letter from a man in New York who works with kids in a special literacy program. He said he likes to challenge his students to achieve and rewards them with signed autographs from people he and his kids see as role models. He asked me to send along an autograph. I was pretty flattered. I was also impressed with this teacher. He knows our young people need to be guided and led.

I got a beautiful letter from the son of this woman I'd been in contact with, Thelma in Wisconsin. What a good woman. She kindly gave some money to the defense fund, and after I wrote to thank her, she wrote me again and I wrote her, and we kept writing to each other. This went on for some time. Then I got a note from her son saying that Thelma had some health problems and was recovering. He told me they were reading my book *Field of Flight* to her. I got a kick out of that. He thanked me for being a friend to his mother. Remember, he signed off, "Our gracious Lord is with you, your family, and our country."

Thelma must be a great mother. The actions of her children show it. Her son and daughter were there to take care of her when she was recovering from an illness. And they read to her. And then her boy wrote to thank someone he never met for being good to his mother. That's a man with good manners he only could have learned from her. So, here's the son living the example his mother set. Just think of what the holidays must be like with that family in a home like that, with so much love and concern for each other.

I got a great letter from a wonderful young man, a fourteen-year-old named Lawrence. He typed it out on his computer.

"I wanted to write because I really do think you inspire a lot of people and still do, and you should know that. I learned you never gave up and that's important. I will never give up on school and I know my family is really important in helping me become a better person."

There's a young man headed for success. I'm honored that he says I inspired him, but the big thing is his respect for his family. If you know teenage boys, they don't often get too sentimental about stuff like mom and dad. But this young man says they're helping him become a better person. At age fourteen he already knows the key to success—when you have your family behind you, anything is possible.

One of the most memorable letters I received was from a young man who grew up in my hometown, Middletown, Rhode Island. He knew my family and Lori's family too. He remembered us and our brothers and sisters and the coaches of the teams we played on in high school. This young man, Allan, joined the Army and wrote that he remembered the afternoon when he was doing push-ups with the rest of his unit and in walks this young officer "starched and spit-shined, Ranger-qualified, wearing 'sky god' master parachutist jump wings, and just back from Operation Urgent Fury–Invasion of Grenada combat patch on his right arm."

That was me. I'd heard from back home that a local boy was in the area and might appreciate seeing a friendly face, so I dropped by to say hello. I won't lie—I get a kick out of that image of the younger me, Lieutenant Mike Flynn. But what really got me emotional was what he wrote next.

"He didn't have to be there," Allan wrote, referring to me. "But what was for him such a simple, routine thing meant an awful lot to me. You never forget who is there to offer a hand, or a friendly face, or a kind word, when you're in a pickle in life."

And that's what America did for me and my family these last few years. You offered us your hand in friendship, and we were honored by it. Your words of affection and encouragement in the letters, cards, and notes you sent me and my family helped keep us going. They pushed us forward. Your words live with me today and always. They inspire me.

From an Army vet who described himself as a "Kansas farm boy"—"Charge on. Always forward, sir."

"Give the bastards hell," wrote a woman named Mary.

"Warriors know how to fight," a retired Naval lieutenant commander wrote. "Real Americans have your back."

"Stay strong. Don't let the bastards get you down," a man named Tony wrote me from Florida. "I fly my flag every day and pray that God will help you through," wrote a woman named Maria. "Don't give up," wrote another correspondent.

I didn't give up. I won't ever give up.

CHAPTER 14

FRAUD AND CORRUPTION RUN RAMPANT

SULLIVAN WOULDN'T LET ME GO

From the moment President Trump appointed William Barr, I was praying the attorney general would see the corruption at the Department of Justice for what it was and that he'd do the right thing for me and my family. Sidney Powell sent him a letter around the same time we pulled my guilty plea detailing the corruption surrounding my case. It was a huge risk, but it paid off. In January 2020, Barr named the US attorney in the Eastern District of Missouri, Jeffrey Jensen, as a special counsel to examine my case. We weren't exactly clear about the details of his appointment nor if it would make a difference, but we knew we had to keep fighting. We were grateful to Barr for appointing this honest man, but by that point we knew that we couldn't count on that to win the day for us.

A little-known fact is that in April 2020, my legal team was asked if I would accept a pardon, but I turned it down. I didn't know the DOJ would dismiss my case the next month, but given the sheer abundance of evidence that had come out publicly and had been turned over to our team, Lori and I were confident that my case would eventually be dismissed. My lawyer Jesse Binnall later said he appreciated the courage it took to make that decision, but Lori and I had faith that the truth would come out. And thanks to people like acting Director of National Intelligence Richard Grenell, his deputy Kash Patel, and later John Ratcliffe as DNI, as well as Jeff Jensen declassifying documents hidden by the FBI, DOJ, and others, it finally did.

Jensen had also served as an FBI agent and started going through the bureau's records of its investigation of me. Among other documents, he found one showing the FBI was prepared to close Crossfire Razor, but after the January 5, 2017, Oval Office meeting with Obama, the FBI kept my case open. Jensen later said in a statement, "Through the course of my review of General Flynn's case, I concluded the proper and just course was to dismiss the case." He further stated, "I briefed Attorney General Barr on my findings, advised him on these conclusions, and he agreed."

And on May 7, the Justice Department withdrew its case against me. US Attorney for the District of Columbia Timothy Shea wrote in a court filing that "the government is not persuaded that the January 24th, 2017, interview was conducted with a legitimate investigative basis and therefore does not believe Mr. Flynn's statements were material, even if untrue." He concluded that "continued prosecution of this case would not serve the interests of justice."[88] Corrupt DOJ prosecutor Brandon Van Grack withdrew from the case, apparently in protest and soon after resigned from the Justice Department.[89]

Barr told the media the DOJ had to dismiss the case because prosecutors could not establish that a crime had been committed. "People sometimes plead to things that turn out not to be crimes," Barr said.[90]

When he was accused of doing Trump's bidding, he said, "No, I'm doing the law's bidding." He said he was prepared for the attacks coming his way about the decision and added that he thought "it's sad

---

88 *United States v. Michael T. Flynn*, United States District Court for the District of Columbia, Case 1:17-cr-00232-EGS, Document 198, filed May 7, 2020, p.13, https://static1.squarespace.com/static/5e80e0d236405d1c7b8eaec9/t/5eb4b4abfa9e604b19e3cae4/1588901092641/Doc.198+Flynn+Governments++Motion+to+DISMISS+against+Michael+T.+Flynn.pdf

89 Dareh Gregorian and Tom Winter, "Justice Department Drops Case against Ex-Trump Adviser Michael Flynn," NBC News, May 7, 2020, https://www.nbcnews.com/politics/donald-trump/justice-department-drops-case-against-ex-trump-adviser-michael-flynn-n1202286.

90 "Attorney General William Barr Says What Michael Flynn Did "Was Not a Crime," *CBS Evening News*, May 8, 2020, https://www.cbsnews.com/news/michael-flynn-case-dismissal-william-barr-attorney-general/.

that nowadays these partisan feelings are so strong that people have lost any sense of justice."

That turned out to be a good description of Judge Emmet Sullivan—even after DOJ withdrew the case, he refused to dismiss it. It seems he was prompted by forces outside the law, namely Barack Obama.

The very day after DOJ withdrew its case, the media published details of a phone call between Obama and former associates in which he talked about my case.

"The news over the last 24 hours I think has been somewhat downplayed—about the Justice Department dropping charges against Michael Flynn," Obama said in the call.[91] "And the fact that there is no precedent that anybody can find for someone who has been charged with perjury just getting off scott-free. That's the kind of stuff where you begin to get worried that basic—not just institutional norms—but our basic understanding of rule of law is at risk. And when you start moving in those directions, it can accelerate pretty quickly as we've seen in other places."[92]

The journalist who was given the leaked call was Michael Isikoff, a leftist who'd already played a big role in promoting Russiagate.[93] It was obvious Obama had made it public as an action message to his faction, including Sullivan. And the message is utterly insane. His allies in our intelligence agencies framed me as a Russian spy, leaked classified foreign intelligence intercepts, and falsified official law enforcement records to charge me with lying to the FBI. And he's saying the rule of law is at risk because the Department of Justice dropped its Stalinist case against me. The forty-fourth president of the United States is conniving, vindictive, and weak. He was any-

---

91 "Obama Leaked Phone Call Transcript: Talks Michael Flynn & Trump Coronavirus Response," *Rev Blog*, n.d., https://www.rev.com/transcripts/obama-leaked-phone-call-transcript-on-michael-flynn-says-rule-of-law-is-at-risk.

92 Michael Isikoff, "Exclusive: Obama Says in Private Call That 'Rule of Law Is at Risk' in Michael Flynn Case," Yahoo! News, May 8, 2020, https://www.yahoo.com/news/obama-irule-of-law-michael-flynn-case-014121045.html.

93 Isikoff, "Exclusive: Obama Says in Private Call That 'Rule of Law Is at Risk.'"

thing but a "leader." Why someone I've never met was so determined to destroy me and my family and divide the country is beyond any measure of decency.

And yet it seems that Sullivan acted on his advice. Sullivan decided he would prosecute the case against me that the Justice Department dropped. He named a former judge named John Gleeson as a "friend of the court" (amicus curiae) to basically represent the prosecution. What's even more bizarre is that Gleeson believes that because I'd withdrawn my guilty plea, I might have exposed myself to perjury. Where did he get that idea? I think that theory was inspired by none other than Obama. He said in that phone call I was charged with perjury, but I wasn't, it was lying to the FBI. And yet days after Obama's dog whistle, here comes Sullivan's court-appointed prosecutor exploring perjury charges. This judicial "prosecution" is unprecedented in US history. Sullivan stepped outside the law and refused to allow the American justice system to function properly.

This was a violation of my due process. And with the judicial branch deciding to prosecute the case against me that the executive branch dropped, it was also a violation of the separation of powers.

My lawyer Jesse Binnall explained it as clearly as anyone. "To take away somebody's freedom through the criminal justice system, you have to have agreement among all three branches of government," he told a journalist. "You have to have the legislative branch that passes a law that clearly regulates acts and behavior. Then you have to have the executive branch that decides that particular conduct is worthy of prosecution, and then you have to have the judicial branch to sit impartially, listening to both sides to decide whether the is evidence beyond a reasonable doubt that the law was broken, often through a jury trial, and then, if so, deciding on the appropriate and proportional punishment."

Yes, Emmet Sullivan effectively took off his robe, stepped across the aisle and started acting as a prosecutor. And there was more to it, said Jesse. "One of the reasons that the Justice Department dropped the charges is because there was no violation of the law. So, in essence, Sullivan was also acting as the legislature. He saw someone that he didn't like, with political beliefs that he clearly detested, and he decided that he was going to pursue him using the criminal justice system, even though no law had been broken. Even though there was no law that prohibited the conduct, he just decided that it was wrong and that it should be punished. So really, he was acting as the legislature as well. He just completely ignored our entire separation of powers."

Jesse said that the late Supreme Court Justice Antonin Scalia used to talk about the importance of separation of powers. "He would explain that every two-bit dictatorship has a Bill of Rights," said Jesse. "He would read aloud from this document written in beautiful prose that just sounded great from a human rights perspective, and then Justice Scalia said, 'that's from the bill of rights of the Soviet Union.' His point was that everybody has a Bill of Rights. It means nothing unless you have separation of powers to enforce it. And that's what Sullivan completely disregarded in his handling of the Flynn case."

Sullivan believed that his politics were more important than his duty as a judge. "When he put on that black robe, he had a duty of impartiality and a duty to do justice," said Jesse. "But he didn't do that. Not in this case. If Emmet Sullivan wanted to be an advocate, which is perfectly fine, he should have stayed as a lawyer where he could fight and advocate. But he decided to become a Judge. He chose no longer to put his beliefs and interests at the forefront but to do justice impartially to everyone who appeared before him. The unfortunate thing is that for many years, he did take it seriously and he could have left the bench with a storied career of someone who did justice. Instead, his legacy will not be as an impartial judge but a politician in a bad black dress who had a gavel in a courtroom and decided to pursue his political interests against General Flynn."

And Sullivan, said Jesse, had his eyes on the political calendar. "The judge thought that Joe Biden was going to win the presidential election and then, one of two things would happen. Biden's Justice Department would change course and look to re-prosecute General

Flynn, or President Trump would be forced to pardon him. The fact is that Emmett Sullivan did not want to have to sign a dismissal showing that General Flynn was innocent. So, he took his time and waited for the presidential election."

I suspect Obama was also looking ahead to the election. Had Sullivan dismissed my case like he should have, I could've jumped onto the campaign trail to help the president. Or maybe I'd have rejoined the administration.

ELECTION SEASON

As it was, I didn't participate in any rallies or political events during the 2020 campaign season. I was too busy fighting the judge who refused to follow the law.

I saw Trump's opponent as a weak candidate, and he probably wasn't their real first choice, but the Democrats have very limited options. Obama backed Joe Biden for the same reason he'd supported Hillary Clinton—because they had total control over him like they had over her. When Trump won, their plans to take total control over America were disrupted. Biden had to win or else Obama's project to transform America would be entirely derailed. Of course, Biden was also the source of my problems. He was at the January 5 meeting and suggested they charge me with the Logan Act.

Around this time, I learned that Biden's brother Jim, and his wife, Sara, had gone to Turkey, where they visited one of the Flynn Intel Group's former clients, Ekim Alptekin. Mueller's special counsel team had pressured Ekim to give them something to use against me, so they could pressure me to give up Trump. But Ekim refused. He told a journalist he briefly considered it. He said that "legal bills were piling up. I couldn't work or travel, but then I thought about what my father told me: You're only a man if you have principles, and it's only a principle if you apply it when it doesn't suit you."

That's an honorable man right there, and he's paid a steep price for his honor. As he told the journalist, he's under a DOJ indictment for making false statements to the FBI and charges related to illicit foreign influence. He hasn't left Turkey for fear of extradition and can't visit his children at their school in the Netherlands. His legal bills are in the millions of dollars, while banks have pulled the plug on his investments, in some cases closing his accounts.

If Ekim is such an outlaw, why did Jim Biden and his wife meet with him in Turkey?[94] In fact, Ekim told the Turkish press it was more than that. He organized meetings for them and paid for their stay at a five-star hotel, The Ritz-Carlton. He wasn't trying to curry favor with the Biden clan, that kind of hospitality is just part of Turkish culture. But why was he indicted for a totally aboveboard contract with Flynn Intel Group, and not only did Jim Biden meet with him but also had no problem accepting a generous gift from Ekim? And also was Jim Biden working on behalf of his brother to continue to put pressure on Ekim to invent some story about me?

It was clear to me Biden was going to benefit from the lockdowns. Trump's natural setting is outside in the fresh air. He loves being outside. He's a sportsman, a good athlete, and he plays golf all the time. His interaction with big crowds, the give-and-take, is on another level—I was there, I campaigned with him, I saw it. It's something I'll never forget. Sure he's a celebrity and used to performing, but I've seen celebrities on stage before, and they don't have half the energy Trump does. When it comes to showing his love for America and its people, he's not performing—it's totally genuine.

Biden couldn't match that excitement; no one can. So they stuck Biden in his basement looking like the sickly old man he is, and sadly for our country it matched the mood of the moment—America sick at home. It didn't help that the COVID task force was filled with people who hated the president, like Anthony Fauci and Deborah Birx, with

---

94   Duvar English, "White House unaware of meeting between Biden's brother and Turkish businessman Ekim Alptekin," March 6th, 2021, https://www.duvarenglish.com/white-house-unaware-of-meeting-between-bidens-brother-and-turkish-businessman-ekim-alptekin-video-56526

Mike Pence in charge. They leveraged the vice president's lack of leadership ability and used the "pandemic" to put the fix in.

In effect, the anti-Trump forces piggybacked on a Chinese Communist Party (CCP) campaign to disrupt our economy and election. We probably won't ever know if Beijing intentionally released the coronavirus, but once they started to lie about COVID, it didn't matter if they did it on purpose. They lied about its origins, and they lied about its effects, even publishing fake videos of people collapsing on the streets of Chinese cities. That was all propaganda designed to advance the CCP's information operation to terrorize and demoralize us.

The Chinese are masters at fifth-generation warfare. In the late nineties, I attended a distinguished program at the US Naval War College where I met two Chinese colonels, who had just written a still very influential book outlining the CCP's unconventional style of total war, titled *Unrestricted Warfare*. I've spent large parts of my military career studying low-intensity conflict and irregular warfare, as well as serving on numerous battlefields around the world. When the Chinese advanced COVID in coordination with subversive US government agencies and people, I saw right away what they were doing. I was, however, not in a position to say anything (at that time). This use of a form of biological warfare is a function of irregular warfare. Never having to fire a bullet in anger on a physical battlefield is China's preferred mode of warfare.

With their support network in places like the CDC and the global media in full support, China waged unrestricted warfare on America, with terrible results. Instead of holding Beijing accountable for an act of war on the US homeland, the Biden administration has coddled the CCP and ignored their provocations, like when the CCP floated a spy balloon over the entirety of the continental United States. And at the same time, China advances their biological warfare program with the assumption they can do the same again with impunity.

As director of DIA, I had a subordinate organization, the Foreign Medical Intelligence Center, with subject matter experts who closely studied the use of biological weapons in warfare. The Chinese biowarfare program is extensive. When you think about the application of illicit narcotics like fentanyl, that tells you everything you need to know about the use and application of the CCP's biological weapons against their adversaries. Drug a culture to decay and eventually die on its own instead of wasting large and vast resources going to a physical war with them. The Chinese are accomplishing this mission.

By early spring, Democratic Party activists began bringing cases to state jurisdictions in order to change normal voting procedures and legalize election processes that invite fraud, like mail-in ballots and ballot harvesting. Even Attorney General Barr told the media that mail-in ballots were a recipe for election fraud. But, of course, the media gaslighted their audiences and said that Barr was paranoid to be concerned about the new voting procedures. That's when I started to worry that things were not going to go well for Trump in November. And then the summer riots began.

There was no reason for the George Floyd protests to have spun out of control the way they did. Had I still been in the administration, I would have recommended that we consider deploying the National Guard to stop the murder and destruction of American cities. These were not disgruntled young people upset because the criminal George Floyd died. These were activist groups supported by Democrat Party donors and officials, like vice presidential candidate Kamala Harris, who were purposely trying to destroy large swaths of American cities to distract from the bigger play, which was to eventually steal the presidential election.

Warfare is all about distractions and deception. And the Left has mastered those political warfare tenets. When you want to make substantial changes in a system, and there is great opposition to those changes, then create actions and counteractions to accomplish your goals.

Trump's team was not ready for this. He had too many people around him who refused to see the problems for what they were. In fact, many were intentionally subverting him. In his administration, two intelligence agencies, the FBI and Homeland Security, were mounting mass censorship campaigns in partnership with the media and Silicon Valley to keep the truth from the American people. Those actions were unlawful violations of the First Amendment and treasonous, but none of them paid the price for their crimes against the electorate, the Constitution, or the president himself.

And Trump was often poorly served by his senior aides. When Defense Secretary Mark Esper and Chairman of the Joint Chiefs of Staff General Mark Milley publicly criticized the president after his walk through Lafayette Park to show resolve and fortitude in the face of chaos, they were wrong.

When leaders at that level have a difference of judgment or opinion with their boss, in this case the president of the United States, they have a duty and responsibility to speak honestly and forthrightly to their boss about it, behind closed doors. If that disagreement can't be resolved, they have a choice—either resign or follow the boss's orders. Instead, after they joined Trump in that walk, they publicly turned on him. It seemed pretty clear to me they were facing pressure to undermine Trump, and they did.

The same seems to have happened with former Defense Secretary James Mattis, who wrote an open letter claiming that Trump was a threat to the Constitution. It was such a massive episode of backstabbing the president, I believed that Mattis was encouraged by others to do it. He has a great reputation from his time in the military, but often a reputation like that affects judgment. The anti-Trump resistance loved it, but it wasn't one of Mattis's greatest moments.

It was part of a larger rebellion by former officers who took shots at the president. In August two retired Army officers, John Nagl and Paul Yingling, wrote an open letter advising the chairman of the Joint Chiefs of Staff, General Mark Milley, to prepare the military to escort Trump from the White House on January 20. They wrote as if they were warning that Trump might attempt a coup when they were really advising the chairman of the Joint Chiefs to topple Trump. I know both Nagl and Yingling—they write a lot, and write well, but with no accountability to anything but their own egos.

With all the turmoil, I felt Trump was being set up—either with the election, a coup afterwards, or possibly something before the elections. After taking so much bad advice from those around him, Trump was finally getting around to exposing the corruption, thanks to aides like Richard Grenell and Kash Patel. They're two of the real heroes of the Trump administration, and their fight to get the truth out will go down as one of the most important exposures of government corruption in US history. With others empowered to join forces with Ric and Kash, Trump's adversaries couldn't risk another four years.

On Election Night I knew then the fix was in, and Biden would be elected. Shutting down polling places in the middle of the ballot count in Pennsylvania and Fulton County, Georgia, was only one of the most egregious examples of fraud.

Our elections have been riddled with election interference and ballot fraud for decades, so the fraud that scarred the 2020 presidential election was not unique. But the nationwide scale of fraud was something America had never seen before. Both parties are to blame, but in the end, it's our responsibility, We the People, to make sure our elections are honest.

With our complacency, we've all but forgotten that our government was designed to be one of, for, and by the people. If we're too lazy to care, we'll wind up living under a tyranny, just as our forefathers warned. "A republic," said Benjamin Franklin, "if you can keep it."

Take it from me, someone who has suffered the tyranny of our self-appointed and unelected political operatives that permeate Washington, DC, bureaucracies. If we don't fight to preserve our God-given liberties, we will lose them as sure as the sun rises over the Atlantic Ocean and sets over the Pacific.

PARDON OF INNOCENCE

In military operations, the best plan has the most options at the last minute. If you're going to plan for a war, you better have a lot of options right up to the last possible minute.

One of the options I discussed with Sidney Powell was that we consider requesting a pardon, just in case, because we didn't know if Sullivan would ever let go. So, after the election, Sidney put in the paperwork for a request and told me that the president would issue me a pardon.

"This wasn't a normal pardon," said Jesse Binnall. "It wasn't a pardon for someone who had erred in the past, had seen the errors of his way, and went on with his life. It was a pardon of innocence. It was a pardon recognizing that General Flynn was vindicated in this process and never should have been prosecuted in the first place. It shouldn't have had to happen. President Trump should not have been forced to pardon General Flynn, and I hate that Emmet Sullivan's bitter strategy played out that way. But any honest American who'd been paying attention knew exactly what had happened—President Trump pardoned an innocent man."

When President Trump called me to tell me he was issuing me a pardon, I was relieved, but I also felt frustrated—my case had already been dismissed, and the pardon was completely unnecessary.

On November 25, 2020, the White House issued a press release stating: "General Flynn should not require a pardon. He is an innocent man. The prosecution of General Flynn is yet another reminder of something that has long been clear: After the 2016 election, individuals within the outgoing administration refused to accept the choice the America people had made. While today's action sets right an injustice against an innocent man and an America hero, it should serve as a reminder to all of us that we must remain vigilant over those in whom we place our trust and confidence. To General Flynn and his family, thank you for all your great service to our nation!"[95]

When Trump and I spoke about the pardon, we laughed like two old friends speaking again. We had spoken only one other time since I left the White House, and that was briefly when he called to congratulate me after the DOJ dismissed my case. That was a very short-lived celebration.

On pardon day, he said now you're the cleanest man in America, and the persecution against you and your family should be over. I laughed and said, "No, Donald, the persecution is just beginning." He laughed and remarked that this judge would not let go of me. "I don't know what his deal is, but for some reason he doesn't like you." Then the president said that this pardon should shut everything down and allow me and my family to get back to a normal life.

I thanked him, asked him how he was doing, and let him know that soon I would reach out and stop by to thank him in person. It was a good call. He was very supportive because he saw the corruption for what it was. However, even after the president of the United States issued me a complete and full pardon, Sullivan waited nearly another month to finally do something he should have issued many months earlier: dismiss my case from his courtroom. He truly turned out to be a vindictive, small-minded man.

My family and I were relieved, but we were also frustrated and still angry about what had happened, from the beginning of the FBI's Crossfire Razor investigation to the historical conclusion with an out-of-control judge finally having no choice but to leave me and my family alone. Never before had a federal judge held on to a case after the DOJ dismissed it and, in fact, said no crime had been committed.

The president and I spoke on the phone a few times after that. I wanted to see how he was holding up. He and I have always con-

---

95 "Statement from the Press Secretary Regarding Executive Grant of Clemency for General Michael T. Flynn," the White House, November 25, 22, accessed at archives. gov, https://trumpwhitehouse.archives.gov/briefings-statements/statement-press-secretary-regarding-executive-grant-clemency-general-michael-t-flynn/.

nected, and I was grateful he recognized what my family and I had gone through. Our relationship remains a strong and honest one to this day.

I was also at the White House for a widely publicized, and wrongly reported, postelection meeting with the president and several of his aides, including White House counsel Pat Cipollone. The discussion centered on legal options given by legal professionals, not me. However, knowing how security clearances work, I told the president that contrary to what his lawyers said, he could approve a security clearance for Sidney Powell to review what had happened during the election.

Had I said or done anything out of line, as the media reported, the phony and corrupt January 6 congressional committee would have come after me hard, but they knew I had neither done nor said anything wrong.

What sticks with me about that meeting is that there were few in his closest circles advising Trump on the constitutional and lawful options he had as president. I heard Cipollone disparage the president's opinion on an election-related issue, and I asked him in front of the president, "Do you believe the president won or lost the election?" Cipollone looked down at his shoes silently. Then President Trump said, "Do you see what I have to f***ing deal with?" At that moment, I felt bad for the president—he must have felt lonely.

CHAPTER 15

AMERICA'S FUTURE

LEARNING FROM RUSSIAGATE

My oldest grandson recently texted me an article that discusses my court case and asked me to explain it. I called him and talked him through it. Thomas was ten when he texted me, old enough to understand the truth. We try to shield children from things to protect their innocence, but he's curious. He wants to understand things, which means knowing the truth about things.

He's a smart boy. He lived in Korea for four years while his father, my son Matthew, was assigned there. He was worried about his father when he was deployed to Afghanistan. He knew that I was a leader in the military and then went to work for the president of the United States. And now he's asking me about this event that changed my life, the life of his family, his life, and the life of the country. So how do I talk to him about this?

I tell him the truth. I wrote this book for Thomas and my other grandchildren. I wrote it for their children and for all our children and the generations to come. I leave it as a record of the truth.

I agree with Devin Nunes that Russiagate is something every school child should know about—it's the biggest scandal in US history. When you add the other campaigns targeting Trump and his aides and supporters—including the two impeachments of the president, the January 6 "insurrection," the raid on Trump's home at Mar-a-Lago, the lawfare waged against 2024 candidate Trump, and so on—it's easy to see that Russiagate, and what followed, was a criminal conspiracy joining political operatives, rogue elements of the intelligence community, and the media to target not just Trump and his circle but the American people as a whole. It tore the fabric of our society and overturned the norms and conventions of our constitutional republic. It ruined lives.

We're living through one of the most volatile eras in American history. It's a divisive moment too.

I ask, how do we teach our kids and grandkids, the rising generation, about Russiagate? But I also recognize that maybe half our great country is teaching something else in schools that will mislead their children. You can bet that for the foreseeable future, public as well as private schools in Democrat-run cities from coast-to-coast will be teaching their children that the forty-fifth president was a Russian spy, and so was I, Michael Flynn, his national security advisor.

Those are lies, and of course it's painful to know I'll be hounded by lies for the rest of my life and after. But here's what's really bad: living in the lie.

It struck me more than once during my ordeal that all these people hunting me, whether they were former colleagues in the intelligence community, political officials, or even the media, lived by lies. And nothing troubles the human soul like a lie, large or small. But then I thought, *What do these people tell their children when some curious kid like Thomas asks his parent a question about Russiagate?*

"Dad, was Donald Trump really a Russian spy, like you said on TV? And General Flynn too? Were they all spies like you kept saying on TV?"

How do they answer that question, and how will they answer it when their grandchildren ask the same question? Will they still lie? "Yes, my child, Trump and Flynn were spies." Or will they tell the truth? "No, son, I just said that on TV because it was part of my job to lie about people in front of large audiences, and Daddy's job pays for our home, your private school, summer camp, and all the nice things your mother and I can give you."

In either scenario, you're lying. Either you're lying to your flesh and blood directly, or you're telling your child that you lie for a living—and that your lies are the economic foundation of that child's life.

To me, that's what hell is—living enslaved to a lie. I never had to worry about that, and I never will. And my heart goes out to all those American kids whose parents built their moral foundations on sand. They'll either grow up lying like their mothers and fathers, or they'll come to hate their parents for lying to them.

So how do we move forward as a nation, with Americans moving in different directions? We're going to have to fight for it. And by that I don't mean we have to fight each other—my story shows there's already been too much of that. I mean that we have to fight for the country we want for our children and grandchildren.

Ever since I was a kid, I was interested in these great powers that no longer exist, like the Roman Empire and the Athenian Empire. They ruled the ancient world and shaped how and what we think and do today. But they no longer exist. So, what happened? What are the signs that a nation is on the way out? What are the indicators of failure? What are the indicators of decline? I believe America may be in a period where we're beginning to see some of those indicators.

So, we should be asking, what are the things that sustain a nation over a long period? And the answer is faith. The power of faith is stronger than anything else in the world. I know from experience.

History shows that they can take your freedom, but they can't take your faith. Tyrants can throw you in jail, as I was almost thrown in jail, or shut you up in even more violent fashion. But they can't take away what you know to be true. Dissidents around the world know this truth—from the Soviet dissidents who helped take down the communist regime in Moscow to the Chinese dissidents who will bring down the communist regime in Beijing. The dissidents were tested by evil, and they survived by faith.

Good always triumphs if good men and women stand their ground and fight, for their faith, their freedom, and their family. I was tested these last several years. War tested me; our enemies tested me. But it was nothing compared to what our own government did to me and my family. I don't know exactly what I'd be if I hadn't been tested like this. I know I would have served President Trump faithfully and loyally as his national security advisor, and I would have risen to every challenge, foreign and domestic, threatening the peace and prosperity of our great nation.

But that wasn't to be. Instead, I was tested in ways I never could have imagined. So what I know is this: I am stronger. Because God was with me and guided me, my faith in God is stronger. Because I nearly lost my liberties, my love of freedom is stronger. And my love for my family, my children and grandchildren, my brothers and sisters, the Tuckerman Avenue Flynns, is more powerful than ever. And my love for our country, and all of you, my American brothers and sisters who stood by me during my hard times, is unbreakable.

ON THE ROAD

A woman said to me not too long ago that what she appreciated most about me, and Lori and our family, is that we maintained our dignity. It really struck me when she said that. I never thought about it like that before. We think about our reputation or integrity or our skills or whatever, but we don't often think about our dignity.

I think a lot of people expected that after my pardon I'd be vindictive and mean-spirited. There's always a part of every human that wants to fight back like that. They tried to destroy my life, after all. They knew that I was innocent and wanted to put me in jail anyway. If I didn't confess to a crime I didn't commit, they were going to go after my son too. So, I had reason to be angry. I could have lost my way, easily. And who knows how I might have turned out if I hadn't decided that I was going to let God run things.

I told myself, *I'll let God run this test that I'm going through. If I'm strong enough, it will all come out fine in the end.* At the end of the day, the truth will come out. It always does. And I think that's where dignity comes from. It's our internal strength. And the source of our strength, as individuals and as a country, is faith.

It was the source of our forefathers' strength, and it's the source of ours too. But for one reason or another we seem fearful of acknowledging that. Some people are embarrassed by it. They think we've moved past God and into an age where we don't need the principles established by faith any longer.

The hard times I've had these past several years have given me time and reason to reflect on our country and our cause. My thinking has been clarified and sharpened by my conversations and correspondence with hundreds of thousands of Americans, maybe by you. We have to return to our roots as a nation, return to our foundations. And we have to look to each other for the strength that comes from fellowship.

Since early 2021, I've been traveling the country for public-speaking events and private meetings. I'm on the road a few times a month and have been across the country many times now. I know what it's like to be on the road from my days in the military, so it is not unusual to be deployed on a mission. My mission now is to help renew our great country.

In March 2021 on one of those trips, I met Clay Clark, a wonderful young man from Tulsa, Oklahoma. Clay is one of the hardest-working people I know. He reminds me a lot of the great young leaders I met during my military career. We immediately connected, and we discussed pulling together a tour to go across the country to rally patriots of all stripes, colors, and backgrounds to send a simple message of hope. We wanted to let the Americans who sometimes worry about our future know that they're not alone. There are millions of Americans like them, and once they realize that we're in the majority, there's all the hope in the world.

Our first event was in Tulsa, a beautiful city with some really great people. We drew approximately 10,000 people, and Clay and I were amazed. We knew that Americans were hungry for the message we brought and eager to meet other Americans who felt the same. But this was something else. At first, we thought we'd only travel to a few places, but the energy of our audiences inspired the "Reawaken America" tour. Since that first event, we've been to nearly twenty-five cities, towns, fields, churches, and other places for our "Reawaken America" events.

The people who attend our rallies are really special. Some have become close friends. People who attend can see for themselves they're part of a large grassroots movement of patriots who stand firm in their faith, fight for their families, and are committed to making America great again from community to community.

I like to say that local action makes national impact. What I mean is that it's time for us all to step up. We're going to have to make sacrifices for our country, and Americans get that. They know it's not just the members of our armed forces who make sacrifices by serving America. If we want to preserve our liberties, it's up to us, We the People, to get out and fight.

America is going through a major transitional period. We are living in a meaningful time, and it's time to remember our roots as a people. Americans don't despair; we wake, and we rise. We commit to do even more for our loved ones, our communities, our houses of worship, our school boards, our town councils, or our county boards. Commitment strengthens our resolve and draws others to our side—everyone wants to be with a winner, and we're winning.

In a constitutional republic by, for, and of the people, it's the regular man or woman who will emerge as the hero. America needs those heroes now. At our rallies, people keep coming up to me to say our "Reawaken America" message has inspired them to take an active role, to become a champion in their community. "I'm running for school board," someone tells me, or county commissioner, or "I've signed up as staff (not just poll watchers) in my local Elections Department." If 10 percent of readers do this, it will make a difference. I've tried for twenty-five years. They say I've inspired them, but I get so much inspiration from them I'm smiling from ear to ear at our events.

Americans are special people. We cherish our freedoms, and we know it takes courage and requires sacrifice to keep them. We're what makes America. When you hear foreigners talk about the greatness of America, they're not talking about political institutions, the Democrat or Republican Party, particular presidents, or the Supreme Court, nor even the Constitution or the Declaration of Independence or the Gettysburg Address—they're talking about the character of the country, us, the American people.

I speak as one who felt your love and strength directly. You came to my aid when I needed it. I wanted to thank you for all you've done for me and my family. You give me inspiration and also a message with a mission attached. You said, fight. Fight with us and for us. Fight for our faith. Fight for our families and communities. And fight for our country. I got your message loud and clear.